✶ CAMPAIGN! ✶

Campaign!

THE 1983 ELECTION
THAT ROCKED CHICAGO

Peter Nolan

Campaign!
© Copyright 2011, Peter Nolan

First Edition
ISBN: 0-9708416-8-X   ISBN 13: 978-0-9708416-8-1

AMIKA PRESS
Jay Amberg, President
466 Central Ave STE 6
Northfield IL 60093
847 869 8084
info@amikapress.com
Available for purchase on amikapress.com

Edited by Amy Sawyer

Cover art by Justin Russo, justindavidrusso.com
Author photograph by Nick Lanscioni

Book designed by Sarah Koz in Adobe InDesign. Typeset in New Caledonia, designed by William Addison Dwiggins in 1939, digitized by Linotype in 1982 and published by Adobe. Thanks to Nathan Matteson.

FOR KAREN
"THE GOOD WIFE"

AND THE KIDS
CHRISTINE
MARY
CARA
PATRICK
MATT
& STEVE

Contents

Foreword

MAYBE IT WAS BECAUSE those old Eastern Seaboard cities had outgrown most of their rascals that they fastened their vicarious political fantasies on that upstart metropolis that blossomed in the early 1900s into the most politically fascinating city of the new century.

Or maybe it all began with the weird but shrewd collection of characters who were the early rulers of Chicago. The most colorful of them was Long John Wentworth, who gained nationwide fame and ridicule when he introduced the visiting Prince of Wales to the Chicago City Council in this way: "Prince, meet the boys. Boys, meet the Prince."

There was Carter Harrison, Jr., the only Yale man elected Mayor, and he was first to do it five times. He holds the distinction of being the first Chicago mayor ever assassinated on purpose. His son, Carter Harrison III, became famed in the early 1900s for matching his father's record of five election victories, all two-year terms.

There were the entrepreneurs, such as the city's first mayor, William Butler Ogden, who later became President of the Union Pacific Railroad, a promoter of transcontinental rail service and the man for whom Ogden, Utah, was named. It was in Ogden that a golden spike was driven to commemorate the opening of the first rail line from the Atlantic to the Pacific.

There was Joseph Medill, who was elected under the Fireproof Party banner in 1871 after the Great Chicago Fire. Medill also founded the *Chicago Tribune* and single-handedly horse-traded Abraham Lincoln into the presidency.

But none of these captivated the Eastern and European press like William Hale Thompson, who was Mayor of Chicago from 1915 to 1923 and again from 1927 to 1931. Known as "Big Bill," Thompson was Chicago's last Republican mayor. After four years out of power, in 1927 he reclaimed the mayor's office with the support of Al Capone whose bootlegging operations Thompson had ironically pledged to shut down during the campaign—a promise he lost no time in forgetting. Instead, Thompson set his sights on bigger targets. He declared King George V of Great Britain the biggest enemy of America and promised his supporters that if they ever met, Thompson would punch the King in the nose. Notable events that took place during his tenure included the Pineapple Primary, which earned its name from the number of hand grenades tossed at voting booths in April 1928. The St. Valentine's Day Massacre happened the following year. His political career ended in 1931 when he lost the mayoral election to Anton Cermak, the founder of what would become the last of the big-city machines. When Thompson died in 1944, $1.4 million was discovered in two safety deposit boxes, an event that, despite World War II news, made the front pages of New York newspapers.

Thompson had hurled ethnic insults at Cermak during the campaign, and Cermak, an immigrant from the Czech Republic, had replied: "It's true I didn't come over on the *Mayflower*, but I came over as soon as I could." Cermak was the second Chicago mayor killed in office, but it was a mistake. Cermak was riding with President-elect Franklin Roosevelt in Miami, Florida, in March 1933 when an assassin's bullet intended for Roosevelt struck Cermak. News reports enhanced Cermak's legend when they quoted his last words as, "I'm glad it was me and not Roosevelt." The boys back in Chicago laughed at that one. Despite his short reign, Cermak had put together the coalition of Bohemians, Poles, Germans and Irish that flourished for 50 years as the nation's most powerful big-city machine, and it created the man regarded for 20 years as the nation's most powerful mayor, Richard J. Daley.

Daley, who served from 1955 until his death in office in 1976, was the man who made Chicago "the city that works." It was Daley who was installed as the biggest kingmaker of all when he carried Illinois for Jack Kennedy in 1960 by running up 90 percent majorities in several city wards. (When asked about his chances of winning the Democratic nomination in 1968, Robert Kennedy said, "Daley's the whole ball game.") And it was Daley who, like so many Chicago mayors before, managed to dirty Chicago's image before the whole world by staging the 1968 Democratic National Convention in an atmosphere of anti-war fervor and civil rights unrest that exploded in a wave of nationally televised violence between his police and the young demonstrators who came to Chicago as peace pilgrims. Daley became a scourge to liberals everywhere, but he was as beloved in Chicago as ever, winning reelection in 1971 and 1975 with nearly 75 percent of the vote. And the national press never tired of coming to Chicago to visit his news conferences, hoping for one of his famous malapropisms or a hint of whom he planned to support for President.

Within three years of Daley's death Chicago would elect another mayor who would titillate the national news media, Jane Byrne. She began as the darling of the reformers and Lakefront Liberals, but within weeks she was labeled by columnist Mike Royko as "Mayor Bossy" for her unilateral, dictatorial rule. She fired city workers and appointed board members with such randomness and frequency that the newspapers had hardly interviewed the new officials before they were gone. She went to war with the police and fire departments and with the teachers and the unions. She brazenly pledged her support to President Carter's re-election and held a massive fundraiser for him only weeks before she endorsed Senator Edward Kennedy's challenge against Carter. She did her best to anger the African American community by booting black members from the Chicago Housing Authority Board and the Board of Education. She viewed herself as invincible, and she was sure of it when two outcasts challenged her in the 1983 primary.

One was Richard M. Daley, son of the late mayor and persona non grata at City Hall during Byrne's reign, despite his election as State's Attorney in 1980.

The other was Harold Washington, an African American U.S. Congressman who had a background in the Illinois Legislature and had been a long-time plodding loyalist in the Chicago Democratic Party. He was a man with a reputation for doing only as much work as the law allowed and less if he could get away with it. Byrne thought that Washington would take black votes away from Daley, whose family still had loyal boosters in the African American wards, and that Daley, with his newly minted appeal to the lakefront crowd, would split the vote of the liberals away from Washington.

It didn't happen that way. After the ballots were counted a Chicago divided between joy and shock woke up to learn that Washington, a black man, had won the Democratic primary and was poised to be the next Mayor of Chicago, since no Republican had won the job since 1927.

But this time the Republicans had a reputable candidate, Bernard Epton. He was a state legislator and well respected by both parties. And they had an issue that made the 1983 mayoral contest the most historic of all: race.

In *Campaign!*, veteran newsman Peter Nolan, who covered all the players in the 1983 contest, has written a first-hand account of not only the key participants, the candidates and their top supporters, but also of relatively unknown election workers who invested their time and passions in a way not seen since in Chicago politics. He uncovers the story behind the timely leaking of medical records that brought into question Epton's mental capacity at a time when it appeared he might win, and he details the bitterness that racial divides throughout the city—on all sides—brought to the campaign. The "council wars" that ensued during Washington's first years in office, which caused the *Wall Street Journal* to dub Chicago "Beirut on the Lake," seemingly continued the discontent of the election outcome and quickly overshadowed its historic nature.

Anyone interested in Chicago history or Chicago politics will enjoy the first-hand accounts of the 1983 campaign. Nolan does not shy from inserting himself into the story where it warrants. His tale of being recruited by Epton as potential City Hall press secretary is only one of the anecdotes that reflects on how unusual the campaign seemed. But in retrospect, it was, after all, a Chicago mayoral election, and no two of them were ever the same.

This is a book that every Chicago politician ought to keep under his pillow and a book that every Chicago journalist should keep on his desk. There is never enough history, and this is a nice slice of it.

—F. Richard Ciccone
Author of *Daley: Power and Presidential Politics* and *Mike Royko: A Life in Print;* former Managing Editor of the *Chicago Tribune*

Acknowledgements

T HERE ARE MANY PERSONS to whom I am grateful for helping make this book possible. Dr. Robert Boone of Young Chicago Authors got me involved in a writers group a few years back
that rekindled my interest in writing. He also connected me with
Jay Amberg of Amika Press, whom I thank for publishing this book.
I'm thankful for the great job of editing by Amy Sawyer and John
Manos, the nifty design work of Sarah Koz and Justin Russo, and
the fine index by Steve Seddon.

Frank Whittaker, Vice President of News for NBC 5 Chicago,
was generous in supplying me with many recorded news stories
from the period. So was V.J. McAleer of WTTW-TV, Channel 11,
which televised many debates of the campaign of 1983.

In writing the book I relied on many sources. Much of the information came from news accounts and commentaries I wrote for television before, during and after the campaign. I also reviewed hundreds
of clippings from Chicago's newspapers: *Chicago Tribune, Chicago
Sun Times, Chicago Daily News* and *Chicago Daily Defender.*
Several books on the topic were of significant help in seeing the
overall picture. Those not cited herein included: *The Memoirs of
Richard Nixon; Don't Make No Waves and Don't Back No Losers*
and *We Don't Want Nobody Nobody Sent* by Milton Rakove; *Chi-
cago Divided: The Making of a Black Mayor* by Paul Kleppner; *The
Making of the Mayor: Chicago 1983,* edited by Melvin G. Holli and
Paul M. Green; Gary Rivlin's *Fire on the Prairie; Fighting Jane* by
Bill and Laurie Granger; *American Pharaoh* by Adam Cohen and

Elizabeth Taylor; and *Harold Washington, the Mayor, the Man* by Alton Miller.

I also reviewed many television programs dealing with the subject, including PBS programs "The Last Boss" and "Eyes on the Prize II: Back to the Movement." Steve Brown was generous in sharing his extensive video library from the period.

A special thanks to retired *Tribune* editor and long-time friend, Dick Ciccone, for writing the foreword to this book.

My old NBC producer, friend and mentor, Joseph P. Howard, was always available as a sounding board on facts and incidents. Dick Kay, the retired Political Editor at WMAQ-TV, opened his large vault of information on Chicago politics. Ted Elbert and Stewart Dan, retired NBC News producers, helped me to gain information from the network. Mike Leonard of NBC's "Today Show" was kind enough to read the manuscript and offer comment. James B. Strong, retired city hall reporter for the *Tribune*, knew much more than he ever wrote, and he shared some of it with me. Hugh Hill, an old colleague from Channel 7, gave some interesting tidbits. Valuable technical advice was provided by Charles Walker, a retired NBC engineer.

Bill Cameron of WLS Radio, the long time City Hall reporter, provided me with his recollections of the campaign of 1983 and also some great recordings of Mayor Washington called "Remembering Harold."

Bob Boone, Jay Amberg, John Manos and Joe Howard, all mentioned earlier, were members of my writers group. I'd like to thank the other members of that group, Chuck Chad, Tony Mitchell and Elliott Goodman. They all reviewed early portions of this book and provided good advice and suggestions.

Many others were generous with their time and valuable information. They included former State Representatives Dan Houlihan, Pete Peters, Charles Fleck, Al Ronan, and Judy Erwin, former State Senators Tim Degnan and Jeremiah Joyce, former Commissioner Ed Kelly, and Terry Durkin.

Over the years I've been blessed with many Chicago friends, all native to the territory, who've given me a better understanding of the town and its politics. These include: Mike Houlihan, John Sevcik, Bill Crawford, Dan O'Brien, Chuck Pierce, Charles A. "Pat" Boyle, Judge Lou Garippo, Bob Rice, Frank and Jack Reynolds.

My brother Mike Nolan offered advice and encouragement on a regular basis.

Thanks to the many staff people who helped me at the Harold Washington Library, The Richard J. Daley Library of the University of Illinois at Chicago, the Newberry Library and the Chicago History Museum. I want to thank David Schaefer, computer aide and the wonderful research staff at the Glenview, IL, public library.

I also thank everyone who was interviewed for this book in recent years and long ago.

Introduction

BARACK OBAMA was a young man, only twenty-one at the time. But he must have known what was going on in Chicago. He had to. It was a major development in the scheme of things that would change his life forever. His buddy David Axelrod was there, right in the thick of it. He had the mustache too, and he was very young. He was a hotshot new reporter for the *Chicago Tribune,* fresh out of the University of Chicago. He seemed to be everywhere in the campaign, his byline appearing almost every day in the *Trib.* The kid was learning about race and politics. He would become a premier political consultant and the maker of a president.

It was 1983, the time when the African American voter came alive in Chicago. Oh, the black man had a right to vote in America. The voting rights act of the Johnson Administration had settled that. And yes, some blacks had been elected mayor in big cities: Carl Stokes in Cleveland, Richard Hatcher in Gary, Indiana, Coleman Young in Detroit and others. But many of those cities were in decline, torn by rioting and unrest. Whites had fled those cities.

Chicago was different. Chicago was a booming place. There was some white flight, but a large portion of the white ethnic population had held its ground. So it was a city deeply divided by race. The geographical dividing lines were major streets. And you could drive along one of these thoroughfares and see it. The Polish, the Irish, the Italians are over there. The brothers are over that way.

Blacks were part of the Democratic Machine in Chicago. They had a slice of the pie. But for many, the feeling was, "The boss man has given us some nice scraps from his table." African Americans came out to vote, but it was a controlled Machine vote and a kind of apathy had settled over the rest of the population. Things were still the same and the "white man was still a bitch with his shit" in Chicago. So, while the Democratic Party got the vote it wanted, everybody else on the South Side and the West Side stayed home. Things were about to change.

I'm standing on the street on the near Northwest Side of Chicago when I see Bernie Epton approaching me. He has just finished a news conference about his plans to improve housing and schools. There must be close to a hundred photographers and reporters dispersing and now here's Bernie coming toward me.

It was early April and still overcoat cold in Chicago. Bernie was running for mayor. Can you believe it? A Jewish Republican from the intellectual neighborhood around the University of Chicago and he's a nose hair away from winning the election just a couple of weeks away. Now he's walking my way and I'm a little nervous because there's still a lot of media around and I'm trying to figure out what he wants with me.

The news media had come from all over the world to cover this wild campaign. Just that morning a reporter from Australia rushed up to me: "Is he really as big a racist as they make him out to be?" I told him I didn't think so, but by this time I wasn't sure what was going on. Bernie was being portrayed as a racist; there was no doubt about that. It didn't help that his campaign had come up with that nasty slogan: EPTON, BEFORE IT'S TOO LATE. What the hell was that all about? Most African Americans and many others took it to mean: EPTON, BEFORE IT'S TOO LATE AND CHICAGO HAS A BLACK MAYOR. Now Bernie was in front of me.

"Pete, how much money do you make?"

"What?"

"I want to know how much you make. Are you under a contract to NBC?"

"Bernie, what the hell are you talking about? Why are you asking me this?"

"Peter, I'm going to win this election and I want to hire you as my press secretary. The city can't afford to pay you what NBC is paying you but I'll make up the difference from my own pocket. If I get elected I've got to have people around me I can trust and I think you're that type of person."

"Bernie, I've got six kids. Some of them are still in high school. I'd have to move into the city. There's no way I could do this. And you shouldn't be making an offer like this to me today. I'm a reporter covering your campaign. It's a conflict of interest."

I said that last part loud because several reporters were moving closer to us, all of them on the eario.

Actually, I was flattered by Bernie Epton's offer. I had been in the news business for twenty years and I was becoming disillusioned. We were always trying to tear the politicians down, destroy them, really. It was a badge of honor if you could dig up some scandal on somebody, knock him out of a race, even better if you could get somebody indicted and then, the super bowl trophy, send a politician to jail.

My problem was I liked most of the politicians I covered. Does that sound crazy? I really did. Yeah, there were some bad ones. I'm not that goofy. And I covered enough cases in the federal court to know that on occasion one of them needed to go to jail. But I found most of them were like the rest of us, loaded with flaws, stumbling along, trying to get it halfway right.

Take the candidates for mayor in 1983. They weren't all that bad.

Bernie Epton, for example, the guy who wanted me to be his press secretary. I really didn't know much about him until he ran for mayor. He was in the legislature, and I knew him only as the guy frequently observed leaning back in his big leather chair on the House floor with a hot white towel covering his head. He had suffered from severe headaches for years. One time he passed out on the House floor. Worried colleagues rushed to his side. One of them was Bruce Douglas, a dentist from the North Side of Chicago. "Get that dentist out of here," Bernie gasped as he came around. "I don't need a dentist." Bernie was OK then, just a fainting spell. Oh, yeah, he had a real dry sense of humor. But the headaches continued. The headaches, I thought, may have had something to do with his service in World War II. Bernie had flown 25 bombing missions over Europe and been awarded two Distinguished Flying Crosses. There were many combat veterans serving in the Illinois House with Bernie in the 1970s, including a Congressional Medal of Honor winner, Clyde Choate from Anna, Illinois.

The incumbent in the race for mayor in 1983 was Jane Byrne. She was a real character. When Jane was in office, there were no slow news days in Chicago. In terms of smart and crafty, Jane probably had more raw talent than any of the other candidates. But she certainly had no adequate preparation for managing a city the size of Chicago. And she frequently made the mistake of taking advice from her husband, a former newspaperman, Jay McMullen. Byrne's chances of getting elected mayor in 1979 were close to zero, but a 100-year snow storm greeted Chicago in the new year. The snow didn't start to melt until Election Day in February, and Chicagoans went to the polls to vent their anger at the Democratic Machine and send that crazy little lady with the blonde wig to the fifth floor of City Hall.

I liked Jane. She was refreshing. In contrast to the tight-lipped organization Democrats, Byrne was famous for off-the-cuff proclamations as she walked down the hallway. Usually her remarks made front-page news. Jane Byrne had faced tragedy in her early life. Her first husband, a Marine pilot, was killed while attempting to land his plane at the Glenview, Illinois, Naval Air Station. Jane was left to make her way with a baby girl, all alone. She found some solace in politics, working on the campaign of John F. Kennedy. Eventually she worked her way up to Commissioner of Consumer Sales for the city of Chicago and Co-chair of the Cook County Democratic Party. And, while her critics privately called her bitchy and neurotic, the public seemed to like this feisty woman. Another storm was in her future, a storm brewing in Chicago's black community, as in: We're tired of handouts from the Democratic Party, how about giving us a crack at the big time, it's our turn, baby!

One of the leaders of this movement was Harold Washington, a congressman and former state senator from the South Side. If anybody knew about plantation politics, it was Harold. He grew up with it. His father had been in it. The Democratic organization was his life blood. He even sided with Mayor Daley when Dr. Martin Luther King, Jr., came to town in the mid-60s. But Harold had a mid-life course change and began to denounce machine politics, exhorting the African American community to rise up and become an independent force in Chicago politics. Harold Washington would be a candidate for mayor in 1983.

Harold came with a fabulous smile, quick wit and cool rhetorical style. He too was a World War II veteran who had served in the Army Air Corps in the South Pacific, helping to build air strips on the islands leading to Japan. But he also had some baggage. He had spent thirty-six days in jail for failing to file income tax returns. And the state had once suspended his law license for failing to show up in court for clients who had paid him fees. A friend said these events came at a down time in Harold's life. But he was back now. And newspaper columnist Mike Royko noted that Harold didn't owe the government much money. He hadn't made that much. He just didn't file the returns.

It seemed everybody in the 1983 race for mayor was trying to make a comeback of sorts. So was Richard M. Daley. He was the son of the late mayor, and so far had not distinguished himself. Yes, he had been elected State's Attorney of Cook County recently and had served in the Illinois Senate, but Chicagoans still thought of the late mayor's sons the way columnist Royko had referred to them: Curly, Larry and Moe. These early predictions about the Daley boys would not pan out in future years. They survived pretty well in Chicago following their father's death. One would become a member of President Clinton's cabinet, manage a presidential campaign, and later become chief of staff for President Barack Obama. Another would hold his own as a Cook County Commissioner. A third was a prominent attorney in private practice.

Richard M. Daley opened his political career as a state senator, his election being a mere formality as the son of the mayor in the home district on the South Side. His early years in the legislature were unremarkable. He hung out with slippery characters and pushed some legislation that got his colleagues wondering if he was acting for his father. The *Tribune's* Ed McManus wrote a humorous story about the concern of Senate leaders, all of whom were afraid to call up the old man to ask if young Rich had his blessing on some of this stuff. I can remember approaching him in the capitol in those days. A nice enough fellow but very shy. Even small talk with a reporter made him very nervous.

Daley too would suffer a tragedy that would change his life. A son, Kevin, would be born with spina bifida. During the legislative sessions, Daley would frequently commute by plane every day between Springfield and Chicago so he could be at the hospital with his boy in the evenings. Kevin would survive for two years before the disease finally claimed his life. And Richard M. Daley would become a better senator. He sponsored legislation to improve the archaic mental health system in Illinois and would lead a fight to repeal the sales tax on food and medicine, a feat that would draw ire from then-mayor Jane Byrne.

So here they all were, ready to do battle in the election of 1983 for mayor of Chicago. The candidates would do and authorize things they might never have dreamed of doing. Epithets and nasty innuendoes would be thrown. The race card would fall many times. Medical records would be stolen. On occasion, rocks would crash through the windows of storefront campaign offices. Brothers would turn against brothers and mothers against sons. The political handling business had become a cottage industry by then, out of New York and Washington, D.C. Many of these bozos came to town, weaving their mischief and half-truths. And the news media was spinning out of control. CNN had begun twenty-four-hour news coverage. British-style journalism invaded the United States and the tabloid news shows were firing up. The networks followed with cheap documentaries. The "in your face" style was in vogue, not just in the media, but in politics and business. There was profit to be made in TV news. No longer would it be public service. The crafty political handlers knew what the media wanted: not campaign position papers, but confrontation.

The campaign and the election would shake the city to its foundation and test its citizens. When it was over the political wars continued, causing the *Wall Street Journal* to look out across the Hudson River toward the wasteland, shake its head, and call Chicago "Beirut by the lake."

PART I

After the Mayor Died

✳ CHAPTER 1 ✳

Richard J. Daley

WHEN I CAME TO CHICAGO in 1968, Mayor Richard J. Daley was in his mid-sixties. He was in the prime of his life and his political career. He presided with near absolute power over the politics and government of Chicago and surrounding Cook County, Illinois. Presidents sought his advice and support.

If anyone wanted to write a textbook on how to become a successful politician in America, they would do well to use Richard J. Daley as a model. It took him a long time to get to the top. He was almost fifty-five years old when first elected mayor of Chicago. He had spent the previous thirty years in preparation. Daley had held positions in the county comptroller's office, the clerk's office, the treasurer's office. He had been state revenue director and served in the state Senate. He was an expert in the financial affairs of local government. He knew where the money came from and how it was spent. He also knew politics. Daley had started out running errands for aldermen behind the City Council chambers, worked for a ward committee-man and became one himself. He once ran for sheriff and lost.

Having come up in the era of Mayor Anton Cermak and gangster Al Capone, he also knew about corruption and how it related to government. He knew how taverns got their licenses. But, in his early years as mayor, Daley was viewed as a reformer. He took many powers away from the City Council whose members were known as gray wolves because of their insatiable appetite for graft. Daley was also a builder. He presided over expressway construction projects and a building boom in the Loop unparalleled in any American city.

When I got to Chicago, the turbulent '60s had begun to wear on Daley. Things were happening in America that Daley and his generation could not comprehend. There was a revolution going on in Black America and a war in Vietnam that many Americans, especially the young people, hated. Race riots had shaken many American cities including Chicago. Daley privately opposed the war but publicly supported President Lyndon Johnson's policies. And well he should have. As author F. Richard Ciccone points out in his book *Daley, Power and Presidential Politics,* Johnson viewed Daley as a godlike figure. He gave the mayor virtual autonomy over the expenditure of huge urban renewal grants to eradicate poverty and slums. Daley did not always spend it wisely, further aggravating the city's African American community.[1]

I can remember the Saturday I drove into Chicago for the first time. I was in a 1967 Pontiac Tempest two-door, my wife sitting next to me and four little kids in the back seat, no seat belts, no fancy child seats.

We crossed the Chicago Skyway bridge and headed north on the Dan Ryan Expressway. The Chicago skyline came into view. For a young newsman coming from WKBN-TV, Youngstown, Ohio and, before that, WHLD Radio, Niagara Falls, New York, this was quite a thrill. I had WMAQ Radio on the air, the NBC station in Chicago. A reporter with a distinctly Chicago accent was narrating a story. His tag line: Marty O'Connor, NBC News reporting.

Marty O was a man I would come to know well in the ensuing years. The legendary Chicago newsman was a filing cabinet of Chicago lore. He looked as if his hair had been combed with a towel. He was known to carry two or three bottles of Old Style beer in his coat pocket for the ride south on the elevated train at night. He had a wonderful saying for everything that happened during the day. "You send a goof out on the job, a goof comes back. The water department put a brick on my pay check. Never make bond under a viaduct."

---

1   F. Richard Ciccone, *Daley: Power and Presidential Politics* (Chicago: Contemporary Books, 1996).

It was March 30, 1968. Stan Mikita of the Chicago Blackhawks had just retained his National Hockey League scoring title. A major league pitcher, Bo Belinsky, returned to his Houston Astros team after a brief absence. He had been angered when the team wouldn't let him break training curfew for a big date. *The Confessions of Nat Turner,* the story of an 1830's slave rebellion in Virginia, topped the *New York Times* Best Seller List. In a few days Chicagoans would find out that, in many ways, tensions between white and black Americans hadn't changed much since the nineteenth century. The next evening, March 31, President Lyndon Baines Johnson went on national television to announce he would not seek reelection. The following day, my first day at work, the president came to Chicago to speak to a convention of the National Association of Broadcasters at the Conrad Hilton Hotel.

On Wednesday of that first week in April, Dr. Martin Luther King, Jr., was assassinated in Memphis and there was rioting in Chicago. From our newsroom atop the Merchandise Mart we could see the West Side of the city engulfed in smoke. In the 1960s, broadcasters in many cities had agreements to withhold immediate reports of urban disturbances so as not to fan the flames. But this was different. One of our senior producers, Charles Baker, convinced his bosses to get a waiver of the news blackout so we could warn citizens to avoid the West Side. Unfortunately, many people were injured when they unknowingly drove into the riot area.

It wasn't long before I was looking at news film of happy looters carrying davenports and television sets out of stores along Roosevelt Road. I remember thinking: Do these guys know they're being photographed committing a crime?

That week, Mayor Daley issued his famous shoot-to-kill order: Shoot to kill arsonists and shoot to maim looters. Today such a policy is probably used by most police departments. Deadly force can be used against those who pose an immediate threat to life and limb of the public. But at the time Mayor Daley said it, the African American community and many whites viewed it as just another cruel attack on poor black people by the white power structure.

Two months later, on June 5, Senator Robert Kennedy was assassinated in Los Angeles. The summer of 1968 was just beginning. I was a new writer at NBC News Chicago on the 19th floor of the Merchandise Mart assigned to the ten o'clock news program. It was called the *NBC News Night Report with Floyd Kalber.* Len O'Connor, who filled up the screen like an old Monsignor, delivered caustic commentaries every night. O'Connor, along with Mike Royko of the *Daily News* and maybe a couple of others, had the nerve to criticize Mayor Daley on a regular basis. We overwhelmed the two other network stations in town when it came to ratings, at one time gaining more of a share of the audience than the other two stations combined. There weren't that many breathless stand uppers by reporters in the field, as I recall. This was before the marketing people took over. We were serious about the news. I was very proud to carry the NBC ID card. Peter Nolan, Editor/writer, NBC News Chicago. Underneath, in German, French, Spanish and English, there was a message from Reuven Frank, the President of NBC News. "This identification is for the exclusive use of the bearer, an official representative of NBC News which will appreciate courtesies extended." As a twenty-eight-year-old broadcast journalist, I thought I had arrived.

As the summer came, the hippies and the Yippies began drifting into town in anticipation of the Democratic National Convention which was to be held at the end of August at the International Amphitheater, located a few miles southwest of downtown near the old Union Stockyards. Mayor Daley built some tall wooden fences along the route to the Amphitheater so conventioneers wouldn't be bothered by unsightly industrial or residential areas as they traveled to and from the sessions.

Abbie Hoffman, one of the Yippie leaders, appeared one morning for breakfast at the Lincoln Hotel with the word "fuck" printed on his forehead. The Yippies released a squealing pig in the middle of the Civic Center Plaza. Demonstrators practiced self-defense maneuvers in Lincoln Park. The *Chicago Tribune* reported that the Yippies planned to put LSD in the water supply. It was that way all summer long. The 1968 Democratic Convention and the violence that came with it is well-documented in the Walker Commission Report. In its preamble, the report said that a police riot had occurred in Chicago. But, if read cover to cover, I believe the Walker Commission presents a fair and accurate account of what happened during the convention. Nobody was on the side of the angels in that confrontation.

I spent the summer screening thousands of feet of film of many of these events. In the summer of 1968 there were a few major stories that dominated our ten o'clock news: the Vietnam War, Civil Rights and, of course, Mayor Richard J. Daley. Before I ever saw the man in person, I saw him hundreds of times in the screening room. Richard J. Daley was the epitome of the authoritarian father figure to a generation of young Americans that was rebelling against all authority. Daley represented the "establishment." And the establishment was what the kids wanted to tear down.

I saw Daley in a different light. He reminded me of my father. Physically, Daley looked a lot like my father. Although my dad was probably a little taller, both men were heavy set. Both had that big Irish head with the florid complexion and jowls.

My father, Ralph W. Nolan, had died in 1948, when I was only eight years old. He had been a lifelong Democrat and devoted follower of Franklin D. Roosevelt. Dad was a workers' compensation lawyer by trade. He was a party precinct captain in our neighborhood. He had run for Congress in 1932, losing in a rock rib Republican district north of Buffalo, while Roosevelt swept the nation. My mom said Dad always wanted to be a judge but he never got the nod. During the war the Democrats rewarded him with a small plum, Chief Price Attorney for the Office of Price Administration.

So here I was, a young writer at NBC, observing and writing about Richard J. Daley. Most of my colleagues thought he was a bozo but I liked him because he reminded me of my old man. Richard J. Daley was a man of many moods and faces. He had an infectious belly laugh that some described as a cackle. He could light up a room. Remember that old expression, "if looks could kill"? Daley had that too, a cold stare that many remembered from his youth. Then the voice would lower to a guttural level.

Once, after a news conference in the early '70s, the mayor went after Channel 7 political reporter Hugh Hill. The cameras had just shut down and Daley was about to exit when he spun around and pointed his finger at Hill. The night before, Hill had presented a report on his ten o'clock news. That day, the *New York Times* had said glowing things about the city of Chicago working quite well while New York City was a mess in the '70s. Hill had gotten an interview with the Mayor, who was happy to take the credit and a few bows. However, Hill inter-cut the interview with sound bites of long-time Daley antagonist Alderman Leon Despres who lectured that yeah, the city might be well managed, but it was still racially segregated and neglected its poor, etc. etc. etc.

"I didn't like that back-to-back last night, Hugh," Daley erupted, "with that other fine citizen. And if I'd known you were gonna do that I never would've given you the interview." Hill's face turned as red as his hair.

Then there was the soft side to Daley. In 1971 I'm sent to the Pick Congress Hotel where Israeli leaders are speaking to a gathering of prominent Chicago Jewish families seeking financial support for Israel's war with the Arabs. The Israeli officials are powerful and persuasive. "Don't give us any pledges. We don't have time for that. We're in a life and death struggle. We need cash. Write us a check dated today."

Then they bring out Cook County Sheriff Richard Elrod and some other local Jewish leaders. And finally himself, Richard J. Daley appears on the stage. He speaks in hushed tones, barely audible.

"Ladies and gentlemen, I'm here to ask your support for the state of Israel. I'll never forget the day my father Mike, God rest his soul, came home in 1947. And he put a piece of paper on the table. And he said, 'This is a bond for the new state of Israel and it's never to be cashed because it's a gift from the Daley family to the courageous people of Israel.'"

The room is hushed. As I look around I see women in mink coats dabbing tears from their eyes. Daley exits the stage and one of the Israeli officials comes out to begin asking for donations. A gentleman in the audience arises and says the Goldblatt family will write a check for twenty-five thousand dollars that afternoon. Another person gets up with an even bigger donation and it's still going on when my camera crew and I have to leave. I remember thinking that we Catholics are fools with our nickel-and-dime bingo games and raffles. This is the way to do it. Put all the wealthy people in one room and let them outbid one another. Israel won the war.

One day I returned to the NBC newsroom after covering a Mayor Daley news conference where I was greeted by Paul Frumkin, who was very anxious to know what Daley said. Frumkin was a wise old owl who was the brains behind *Kup's Show*, a late night talk fest on Channel 5 hosted by the highly regarded gossip columnist of the *Chicago Sun Times*, Irv Kupcinet. Frumkin was one of those knowledgeable, well-read men whose office walls were lined with piles of the *New York Times* and an array of other brand-name national and local publications. *Kup's Show* was on late Saturday nights and would include several guests from show business, politics and other fields, sitting around sipping coffee and discussing the events of the day. In the late '60s, a typical panel might include Sammy Davis, Jr., with a rum and coke in his coffee cup and Richard Nixon, who was still trying to become president.

Anyway, on this day, Paul came up to me and wanted to know what the Daley news conference was all about. I looked at my notes. I had written down some quotes and realized I had no idea what they meant. I apologized to Paul and told him I really didn't get what the mayor was saying. I was embarrassed. We had a press release which detailed the subject of the news conference. But as far as what Daley had said about other subjects, I didn't have a clue. Paul insisted I read him what I had written, which I did. He seemed to understand it perfectly. He walked away nodding his head, mumbling, "Yeah, he's gonna get rid of that guy." I soon found out that some of the old timers knew how to translate Mayor Richard J. Daley. My job was easy, though. I'd just write the lead-in. Mayor Daley announced today the appointment of so-and-so as Deputy Superintendent of Streets and Sanitation. During his news conference he was asked about the current controversy involving Chicago School Superintendent so-and-so. Then we'd just run the sound bite and let the public figure out what Daley meant. I do think many of the citizens out there seemed to catch Daley's drift. My colleagues in the newspaper business had a much more difficult time putting their story together.

There was always a mystery surrounding the mayor's public statements. Malapropisms and fractured syntax were terms used to describe things he said. To this day, many Chicagoans remember some of the great ones. One of my favorites: "I never said that and some of you fellas were there when I said it."

President George W. Bush would have loved Mayor Richard J. Daley.

I was amazed at the amount of coverage we gave to the mayor's every utterance, whether it made sense or not. One of my jobs was to chase Daley around with a camera crew to try to capture whatever he said about anything. Often we went to his house early in the morning to wait for him. I was a little squeamish about this. It seemed to me there was something sacred and private about a person's home, even a major public figure like Richard J. Daley. But we did it anyway and Daley was used to it. I quickly found that the mayor didn't like the ambush interview, shoving a mic into his face and blurting out a question. He'd just breeze by with a, "Nice day, fellas," get into his car and be gone. I found over time that if you tried to be polite, the mayor would respond. "Excuse me, Mr. Mayor, can we ask you a couple of questions?" Then he'd stop and talk for a bit. He rarely said anything of consequence but that didn't matter. If you had thirty seconds of Daley, you had something.

We'd also stake him out at his City Hall office, camping out on the ground floor or even in the reception area of his office on the fifth floor. The assignment desk was always anxious about the whereabouts of the mayor. Frequently the two-way radio would blast, "Any sign of the mayor?" "Nothing yet." It was a great assignment. We'd drink coffee, smoke cigarettes and make personal phone calls in an ante room with phones for the press.

If it wasn't some major local issue, our desk frequently wanted Daley's reaction to a major world or national event. Even though the mayor never said anything of great consequence, whatever he said made the ten o'clock news.

"Mr. Mayor, what is your reaction to the renewed bombing attacks on Hanoi?" Daley's reply in very soft tones: "Well we all know these are very difficult times for our nation. And we'll say a prayer for our young men and women in harm's way so that they all come home safely."

Then another urgent call from the assignment desk.

"Did you get Daley? Did you get the mayor?"

"Yeah, we got him."

"What'd did he say?"

"He says he's going to pray for our men and women in uniform."

"Great job! Bring it in here."

And after the lead story on the ten o'clock news, Floyd Kalber would say, "And there was this reaction from Chicago Mayor Richard J. Daley." I'd come to work the next day and someone in the newsroom might say, "Nice work on the Daley interview." I remember thinking, this is pretty easy work. I think I can do this.

In 1972 Richard J. Daley and his hand-picked delegation from Chicago were dumped from the Democratic National Convention in Miami and replaced by a delegation headed by Alderman William Singer and Rev. Jesse Jackson. Daley had failed to comply with new Party rules requiring quotas of minorities, women and young people in the delegations. It was a final crushing blow for the old political warhorse which some thought was a punishment for the 1968 convention in Chicago.[2]

Daley may have been viewed as a villain by much of the country in the late 1960s, an autocrat who was the last of the big city machine bosses. But Chicago still loved him. He won reelection with big majorities in 1971 and 1975. And the man began to mellow in his seventies. While the nation was preoccupied with Watergate and the resignation of President Richard M. Nixon, Richard J. Daley was recovering from surgery to repair a blocked carotid artery, which had caused a minor stroke earlier.

---

2 Ciccone, *Daley: Power and Presidential Politics,* 286.

And he came back with gusto. At a news conference one day a reporter asked if he was mad at a certain candidate who was opposing the Democratic organization in a primary election. "Mad? Mad?" Daley bellowed. "Listen, pal, I'm not mad at anybody. I'm just happy to get up in the morning."

Daley began to be treated as an elder statesman of the party. Governor Jimmy Carter of Georgia put some heavy moves on the mayor as he sought the Democratic presidential nomination in 1976.[3]

Celebrities who came to town sought audiences with the venerable mayor. Frank Sinatra appeared at a news conference with Daley. Secretaries lined the fifth floor hallways to get a glimpse of the crooner. Daley's press secretary, Frank Sullivan, may have been a bit over exuberant when he said, "Can you believe it? Two of the twentieth century's greatest personalities in the same room together!"

Another time he tried to sing a few bars of the Polish version of "Melody of Love" with pop singer Bobby Vinton. Perry Como, John Wayne and Bob Hope were also visitors.[4]

I don't think Mayor Daley will be remembered much as an environmentalist, but he was an avid fisherman and a gardener. At news conferences he sometimes talked about the garden he tended at his summer home in Michigan where he grew tomatoes and cucumbers. "When you're in a garden you're never closer to God," he would say in prayerful tones.

He was intent on cleaning up the long-polluted Chicago River. "Some day, with the help of God, maybe we could all fish in the Chicago River. And maybe we could stock it with perch and coho salmon and bluegill. And maybe we could have barbecue grills at the riverside and some of you fellas could go down there at lunch time with your wives and girlfriends and catch a fish and then cook it right there."

During the height of the women's movement, Daley was asked by a female reporter why women did not hold any important positions

---

3   Ciccone, *Daley: Power and Presidential Politics*, 310
4   Robert Davis, "Running Chicago," *Illinois Issues,* February 22, 1995.

in the Democratic Party of Cook County. "Listen dear, you've got it wrong. Women have always been involved. Why, they run the fine card parties and the fashion shows."

In the 1970s, Richard J. Daley attained what most politicians only dream of: legendary status. It was short lived.

On December 20, 1976, the mayor had scheduled an appointment with his personal physician, Dr. Thomas Coogan, at his office on North Michigan Avenue. While the doctor was out of the room briefly, Daley collapsed and died. Heroic efforts by doctors and paramedics failed to revive him. He was seventy-four years old.[5]

I was sent to the home of Alderman Vito Marzullo in the 25th Ward on the West Side. The old don lamented the loss of his beloved leader in at least two live shots in our early evening news.

The night of the wake I stopped by Riccardo's, a local watering hole for journalists, PR and advertising people. It was crowded. Someone introduced me to Jimmy Breslin, the esteemed New York writer. He seemed a bit shy. I watched him go over to say hello to Mike Royko who was standing at the bar with another man. As caustic as ever, Royko proclaimed loudly, "Did some Irish big shot die? I see a lot of strange turkeys in town."

President Gerald Ford and President-elect Jimmy Carter led the mourners at Daley's funeral mass at Nativity of Our Lord Church on a bitter cold day in Chicago.

On the day Richard Daley died, Mike Royko wrote a column saying Daley "was this town at its best—strong, hard driving, working feverishly, pushing, building, driving, driven by ambitions so big they seemed Texas boastful. In other ways he was this city at its worst—arrogant, crude, conniving, ruthless, suspicious, intolerant."

Daley's talents and shortcomings will be debated for years to come. It seems clear that he loved Chicago, loved his wife and family and had a deep faith in the Catholic religion. At the time of his death Mrs. Eleanor "Sis" Daley told someone, "Not a day went by that he didn't say he loved me."

---

5   Len O'Connor, *Requiem* (Chicago: Contemporary Books, 1977), 15.

In his wallet were found several well-worn prayers including the prayer of St. Francis of Assisi and a prayer by Richard Cardinal Cushing, Archbishop of Boston, called "Slow Me Down, Lord."

Richard J. Daley, during all his years at the top of Chicago, had groomed no successor. There was never a number two person.[6]

And as Royko wrote in that same column the day of his death: "Daley, like this town, relished a political brawl...Well, he's left behind the ingredients for the best political donnybrook we've had in fifty years. They'll be kicking and gouging, grabbing and tripping, elbowing and kneeing to grab all or a thin sliver of the power he left behind. It will be a classic Chicago debate. He knew it would turn out that way and the thought probably delighted him."[7]

---

6   Mike Royko, *The Best of Mike Royko: One More Time* (Chicago: University of Chicago Press, 1999), 102.
7   Ibid., 105.

✳ CHAPTER 2 ✳

Michael A. Bilandic

T**HE MORNING AFTER** *Mayor Richard J. Daley's death I was
sent very early to City Hall to see what was happening. Black
and purple bunting covered the entrance. I felt a little sad as I
entered, knowing that the little old guy with the jaunty step, whom
I had chased so often, no longer would be there. We had waited
for him so many times inside the main entrance. I remembered the
time he had caught us napping. The crew and me sitting on the floor,
having coffee. And he came bursting through the doors, right by us.
Then he must have caught us out of the corner of his eye and he
wheeled around and began laughing wildly. "Say, what happened
fellas, were you taking a little rest period?" Then, before we could
scramble, he was off again, still laughing. He had escaped. All that
was over now.*

    *My camera crew and I rode to the fifth floor and stepped out into
the large foyer leading to the mayor's office. This foyer was 100 feet
long and half as wide. In a moment I noticed another elevator door
opening across the hall and out came 10th Ward Alderman Edward
Vrdolyak and 34th Ward Alderman Wilson Frost. Vrdolyak was a
brash, talented man who had been raised above a tavern in the steel
mill area on the far Southeast Side of Chicago. Frost, a black lawyer
from the far South Side, was a loyal Democratic Party man who was
president pro tem of the City Council. He believed he was the acting
mayor because of Daley's death. He had presided over the Council
during the time the late mayor was recovering from his stroke.*

The two men eyeballed the camera crew and me and then looked toward the mayor's office. I saw something there I had never seen before. There were always two glass doors leading to the mayor's office. But on this day, two sliding oak doors were closed behind the glass. I couldn't remember ever seeing these heavy doors in use before, never knew they were there. But they were closed and you couldn't see inside. Several feet in front of the doors there was a wooden stand with a book to sign for those paying their respects.

At this moment, from the corridor to the side of the doors appeared two men. Thomas Donovan had been the late mayor's administrative assistant and chief aid. Frank Sullivan had served as press secretary. It was obvious who had the keys to the mayor's office. Vrdolyak and Frost did an about face into the elevator and Donovan and Sullivan disappeared.

I don't think we really captured this moment on film. Maybe we got a shot of Vrdolyak and Frost. We would have needed three cameras because the other two men were far down the hall and the lighting wasn't good there. Surely Vrdolyak and Frost must have known right away they were too late. The keys to the office were in the hands of the 11th Ward. Donovan knew where all the patronage jobs and all the skeletons were. There were many events that energized Chicago's black community. This had to be one of them.

Here were two officials of the previous administration, elected by no one, shutting out the president pro tem of the City Council. Wilson Frost had always been loyal to the Democratic Party. He was a classy guy all the way. It was like they said, "We just can't give you the keys, you're a black man."

The city lawyers said only the Council could elect an acting mayor. And so the maneuvering began. I wonder today what would have happened if there had been a confrontation between Frost and Vrdolyak and Donovan and Sullivan. And what if we had captured it on film and put it on television? Chicago's African American community would have been outraged.

Black political leaders were pretty ticked off as it was. Rev. Jesse Jackson, state Representative Harold Washington and others did some heavy lobbying of Council members on behalf of Wilson Frost.

Although he insisted all along that he was the acting mayor, Frost agreed to an arrangement whereby he would be in charge of the City Council and Deputy Mayor Kenneth Sain would run day-to-day city operations until the Council could meet and elect an interim mayor.

On the Sunday following the mayor's death, a group of aldermen including Frost, Edward Vrdolyak, and Edward Burke and top city officials met at City Hall and later at Alderman Burke's law office. A deal was reached. 11th Ward Alderman Michael Bilandic would be elected acting mayor. Frost would become Council floor leader and chairman of the powerful and patronage-rich finance committee. Alderman Vrdolyak would take Frost's place as president pro tem. The Polish block was given a new post, that of vice mayor. The vice mayor would automatically become acting mayor in the event of any future vacancies.

The City Council met on December 28, eight days after Mayor Daley's death. The public section of the chambers overflowed with people. Those who couldn't get seats spilled into the hallway. Activists from the African American community packed the balcony above.

The Council made official the prearranged deal. The problem was no one informed many of the blacks present that Wilson Frost had given up his quest and settled for the number two spot. Some of them banged on the glass windows when a black alderman got up to second the nomination of Michael Bilandic. But all went as planned.

Alderman Wilson Frost spoke at the end. In a chamber not renowned for eloquence, Frost gave one of the great dramatic speeches. He said he understood black leaders wanted him to hold out, but in the end he knew how to count and he simply didn't have enough votes. "It was a suicide mission. If I had done it, what would I bring home to my people?"

There were some appealing traits about Michael Bilandic. He assured everyone on the Council that he would not be a candidate in the special election to be held within six months to fill Mayor Daley's unexpired term. Some of the other aldermen were thinking seriously of making that race. He was also genuinely liked by most of his colleagues.

Mike Bilandic became chairman of the City Council Finance Committee after Tom Keane, Mayor Daley's longtime floor leader, was sent to federal prison. Keane was convicted in October of 1974 in a scheme that involved the buying and selling of tax-delinquent property.

Keane was a brilliant man with a sour personality who ran the financial affairs of the city with total authority, and he had Daley's blessing most of the time. He had tiny eyes and a crooked little smile that seemed to say, "Get ready, we're taking you to the cleaners." If an alderman had the gall to introduce a proposal without his OK, Keane would jump to his feet and sneer, "Lay on the table." A motion to lay on the table meant death to the proposed legislation.

Many aldermen, especially the young ones, objected to his practice of handing out administration legislation the day it was to be voted on so no one had a chance to read it.

So, few tears were shed in the Council when federal prosecutor James R. Thompson nailed Keane on corruption charges and old Tom was shipped off to the federal correctional facility in Lexington, Kentucky, in 1976.

When Keane was released from prison I was sent to cover the event. Keane was out of the place and into a waiting car in the blink of an eye. We barely got a picture of it. Later I interviewed a prison employee who ran the sewage treatment plant where Keane had worked during his stay. "He was the best worker I ever had. He kept perfect records and even docked his fellow inmates if they were even five minutes late for work." But he accepted none of the token pay and asked that it be given to the men.

The City Council scheduled a primary election to fill the unexpired term of the late Mayor Daley for April 19, 1977. The general election was set for June 7.

Michael Anthony Bilandic was 53 years old when he was sworn in as acting mayor of Chicago on December 28, 1976. He was a handsome man with sad blue eyes. Bilandic had served as an officer in the Marine Corps during World War II and had fought as a platoon leader in the battle for Iwo Jima. Still in great physical shape, he had taken up jogging and marathon running. A first-generation

Croatian American, Bilandic was a bachelor who lived with his wid-owed mother, Minnie, along with two brothers and a sister.

Bilandic had been a successful corporate lawyer who became moderately wealthy investing in some of his clients' businesses. He was honest, had a good reputation and had a great knowledge of city government and the budget. He seemed to be the perfect choice to manage the city in these trying times following the death of Daley.

At the time of his swearing in, Bilandic was also in love, perhaps for the first time in his life. Her name was Heather Morgan. She was blonde and beautiful and accomplished. She had recently been named Executive Director of the Chicago Council on Fine Arts after having served as Deputy Commissioner of Aviation for the city. To the media it seemed like an odd match. He was in his mid-fifties; she was in her mid-thirties. He was from the blue collar Bridgeport neighborhood. She was from high society, Lake Shore Drive. But it was the real thing. The couple would marry the following summer.

A funny thing happened in the next few months. Michael Bilandic discovered that he liked being mayor of Chicago. The man who had volunteered to be a caretaker mayor until a special election could be held seemed to enjoy the attention. Celebrities visited him at City Hall the way they had come for the late mayor. The great songwriter Sammy Cahn appeared with him at a press conference and told why Chicago was his kind of town. "When I come here," Cahn said, "I feel I'm in a place that's well governed. In my hometown, New York City, I sometimes want to scream."

There was a strike by the city's grave diggers. Bilandic brought both parties to his office and a settlement was reached.

Other forces were at work to keep Bilandic in the mayor's office. Thomas Donovan, the administrative brain and patronage chief, and the late mayor's sons were of a mind to extend Bilandic's stay. They wanted to protect the interests of the 11th Ward. It was estimated at various times that the 11th held about two thousand jobs in city government. Who else but a son of the Bridgeport neighborhood could be trusted to protect them? Then, of course, there were the mayor's sons. What if one of them wanted to follow their father to the fifth floor of City Hall? It wouldn't be wise to have a stranger keeping the seat warm.

The 11th Ward went about the business of convincing the city's other ward committeemen. These local bosses, who had been regimented under Richard J. Daley so long, saw the wisdom of the argument. Under Bilandic, nothing changes. You keep your patronage. You keep everything you've got. Why rock the boat? And after all, if the late mayor was grooming anyone to succeed him, surely it was Bilandic.

There were other potential candidates. The powerful Congressman Dan Rostenkowski, also the committeeman of the 32nd Ward, let it be known that he was available, as was Ed Kelly, committeeman of the 47th and head of the Chicago Park District. George Dunne, President of the Cook County Board and committeeman of the silk stocking 42nd Ward, said he was interested too. But Dunne was about to be elected chairman of the Cook County Democratic Party. And most of the committeemen did not want the power of both the mayor's office and the Party Machinery to be in the hands of one man again.

The only announced candidate for the special election was 41st Ward Alderman and Committeeman Roman Pucinski, a former congressman and newspaper reporter. Pucinski said he took Mike Bilandic at his word when he agreed to vote for him for acting mayor. "He looked me in the eye and told me he would not run in the special election," Pucinski said, "and I believed him."

Activists in the black community were anxious to have a candidate in the coming race. Two committees were formed; the smaller one included prominent African American businessmen concerned with financial aspects of the campaign. The main committee was charged with recruiting a top flight candidate. The cochairmen were Gus Savage, a community newspaper publisher, and Congressman Ralph Metcalfe, boss of the 3rd Ward and heir to the organization of Bill Dawson, a legendary South Side congressman and political boss. Metcalfe was a local hero. He had won a gold medal in the 1936 Olympics as a relay runner and finished an eyelash behind Jesse Owens in the 100 meter dash. This was the so-called Nazi

Olympics held in Berlin, which proved to be an embarrassment for the German fuhrer, Adolph Hitler, who had proclaimed German Aryans to be a superior race. At the last minute the U.S. coach had substituted Owens and Metcalfe for two Jewish kids on the relay team. It was widely believed at the time that the move was orchestrated by Olympic Chairman Avery Brundage so Hitler would not be embarrassed. One of the Jewish kids was Marty Glickman, who would later become a Hall of Fame sports broadcaster.

The committees seemed to favor state Senator Harold Washington, who had just moved to the Senate from the Illinois House and was making news in a bitter battle for Senate leadership. But Congressman Metcalfe announced that he could not support Washington. An angry Washington immediately announced he was withdrawing his candidacy.

Next, the committees selected Robert Tucker, a federal attorney with close ties to Rev. Jesse Jackson. But Tucker also dropped out of the race. With no viable candidate, the African American coalition threw its support to Alderman Roman Pucinski. There was even talk of a Black/Polish coalition. But that never materialized.

In mid-February, just two months before the primary election, Harold Washington decided to get back in the race. Within a week he picked up the endorsement of a liberal political group, the Independent Voters of Illinois. The endorsement was not unanimous. Leaders of the IVI said they had concerns about Washington's jail term for failing to file income tax returns and the suspension of his law license for collecting legal fees without performing the services.

Less than two weeks after Michael Bilandic's swearing in as acting mayor of Chicago, there were newspaper reports that state Senator Richard Daley, who had succeeded his father as committeeman of the 11th Ward, was behind efforts to draft Bilandic as the party's candidate for mayor in the special election.

Bilandic enjoyed the limelight and he liked being coy about his intentions. "My mother told me never to stand in the way of a draft," he joked to inquiring reporters.

Soon business and labor leaders were encouraging Bilandic to run.

Chicago Daily News columnist Mike Royko was not as enamored with Bilandic. Referring to the acting mayor's promise not to run in the special election, Royko wrote, "He has shown that he has one traditional qualification for the job of Chicago mayor. He can look people in the eye while lying his head off."

Bilandic's 11th Ward handlers kept him looking more and more mayoral and more like a candidate. He was making frequent public appearances and holding more news conferences. One day in early January the city's Commissioner of Consumer Sales, Jane M. Byrne, was scheduled to hold a news conference on coffee prices. The mayor's advisors decided Bilandic should hold the news conference instead and told Byrne to stand aside at the last minute. This decision would be a major mistake. Jane Byrne was a spirited woman quite capable of retaliation.

There was no stopping the Bilandic juggernaut. At the end of January the Cook County Democratic Central Committee endorsed Acting Mayor Michael A. Bilandic as the party's candidate to fill the unexpired term of Mayor Richard J. Daley. The vote was a resounding 47 to 2. Committeeman Roman Pucinski voted for himself. 43rd Ward Alderman William Singer, a lakefront independent who had run unsuccessfully against Mayor Daley in 1975, received one vote.

Bilandic faced five other Democrats in the primary election. In addition to Pucinski and state Senator Harold Washington, Edward Hanrahan, a former state's attorney who had been dumped by the party following a controversial Black Panther raid, Anthony Martin-Trigona, a political gadfly, and Ellis Reid, a black attorney, also appeared on the ballot.

Bilandic won easily with 51% of the vote, getting more votes than the other five candidates combined. Pucinski received a respectable 32%, and Senator Washington came in third with 11%.

I have this memory of Mike Bilandic walking down the middle of the street. He has won the primary election for mayor and is now in the general election campaign. His opponent is a young, good looking alderman from the 48th Ward by the name of Dennis Block who was recruited as the Republican candidate by Governor James Thompson. Block, the only Republican on the council, had seconded

*Bilandic's nomination for acting mayor in December. His chances
are slim to none.*

*On this day I am following Bilandic, who is walking through his
home neighborhood of Bridgeport. A vigorous walk for a vigorous
mayor. Crowds of enthusiastic supporters have lined the streets.
Tom Donovan, the brains of the operation, is walking a discreet
twenty feet behind the candidate. At times, Donovan approaches
Bilandic to point out some people Bilandic knows. Perhaps they
are neighbors or people who have rung doorbells for him. I think
Donovan wants the mayor to go over and say hello to them. But the
mayor seems oblivious. He stays in the middle of the street, waving,
smiling, nodding approval like he's some kind of potentate. Donovan appears frustrated and backs off.*

*I remember thinking: this Bilandic is a nice man and very capable.
He could probably be mayor for a long time. But he doesn't seem
to be much of a politician. There doesn't seem to be much warmth.
And what if trouble comes? What will happen then?*

Michael Bilandic won the June 7 general election with 77% of the
vote. But the campaign had not created a great deal of public interest. Only 38% of the city's eligible voters came out. Dennis Block
politely conceded. He lost every ward in the city including his own
but said he might consider running again in 1979. Block was never
heard from again. The following month, Bilandic married Heather
and began his family life and his new administration. For the next
eighteen months his leadership would be tested frequently.

The day after his election, the new mayor was asked to mediate
another labor dispute. Chicago's taxi drivers had voted to strike the
city's two major cab companies, Yellow and Checker. He went to a
secret meeting with union and company officials at Midway Airport.
The company indicated it might agree to a settlement if it could get
a fare increase of about twelve percent. The fares were regulated
by the City Council and Bilandic said he would support such a hike
if the company could show that its profits had fallen off. Within
a month the strike had been averted and the City Council had
approved the requested fare increases. This action would cause one

of the great political and media brouhaha's of the 1970s. It would be a major distraction to the new administration.

William Griffin was a bright young reporter for the *Chicago Tribune*. He had earned his credentials at the famed Chicago City News Bureau and had served for a time on the City Hall beat. He was a local guy who grew up on the North Side. He was the first young man in his family in a hundred years who did not become a Chicago policeman.

Griffin had written an article that caught the attention of Consumer Sales Commissioner Jane Byrne. She called the reporter to compliment him and soon was calling him on a regular basis. She told him that there was something wrong, perhaps illegal, in the way the City Council had rushed through a fare increase for the Yellow and Checker cab companies. She believed that fraud and conspiracy might be involved. And Mayor Bilandic was up to his ears in it. The young reporter smelled a blockbuster story. He went to see his editors. They told him to drop everything and work this story. William Mullen, a Pulitzer Prize-winning investigative reporter, was assigned to work with him. There was one problem with the story. Byrne was unwilling to go public with the charges. She had a daughter at Notre Dame and she was worried about her job. The reporters researched the story for three weeks but were unable to confirm Byrne's charges through other sources. Their editors agreed that they shouldn't print the story. Griffin called Byrne to tell her they needed more information. Later that day Byrne called to say that Channel 2's Walter Jacobson was going with the story. Mike Royko of the *Daily News* also wrote a column, and the media floodgates opened.

One of the things that Byrne said in her charges was that Bilandic had "greased the way" for the taxi fare increase. Those three words resonated in every story that was printed or broadcast in the future.

There was another clinker in the story. The *Tribune's* attorney, Don Reuben, was also the attorney for Checker and Yellow cabs. Byrne was telling everyone that part of the Bilandic scheme was to have Reuben get hold of his people at the *Tribune* and kill any negative stories about the fare increase.

Reuben was a high powered, aggressive, influential and abrasive lawyer. In addition to the *Tribune,* his media clients included *Time* Magazine and WMAQ-TV, the NBC-owned-and-operated station in Chicago. Channel 5 reporters and writers were often told to call Reuben about a particularly sensitive story and run it by him. Reuben's standard advice: "If you put that on the air they're going to sue you and I hope they do." Fortunately, news executives at NBC would sometimes overrule him.

Eventually Byrne went public with her story. She met with the United States Attorney, Thomas Sullivan. The *Tribune* had egg on its face. It printed articles explaining how it handled the story. Top editors were quoted. They said they believed they had done the right thing and denied that Don Reuben had anything to do with their decision. Reuben also denied that he tried to influence the paper. Bill Griffin was called before the editorial board and was asked a lot of questions. It was uncomfortable. He was looked at suspiciously by many of his colleagues.

In addition to the U.S. attorney's office, the Federal Trade Commission was looking into the matter. Cook County State's Attorney Bernard Carey, a Republican, jumped into the fight with his own investigation. Even the City Council began a probe.

Jane Byrne took a lie detector test and passed. Her test was paid for by the *Chicago Daily News,* which got an exclusive on the story. Byrne had been dating Jay McMullen, the longtime City Hall reporter for the *Daily News.* Mayor Bilandic took his own test and passed. Critics said neither one of them answered the right questions. The same day he passed his test, Bilandic fired Byrne.

In the end, nothing much came of the great taxi cab fare scandal. It may have had the look and the smell of an old-fashioned slippery Chicago deal, but all the investigations could never pin anything on anybody. Bilandic plowed ahead. *Tribune* reporter Bill Griffin was vindicated but, understandably, he didn't want to have much to do with Jane Byrne after that. Byrne was out of a job and she was ready to do battle.

In 1975 I was offered *a job as political reporter for WBBM-TV (CBS) and I took it. I remained at Channel 2 for three years and then returned to NBC, where I had the opportunity to do commentaries on the ten o'clock news.*

My three years at CBS were marked by significant events including the death of Richard J. Daley and the beginning of the post-Daley era. There were changes happening in television news. Dual anchors were in vogue and more and more women were coming into the business. Producers wanted reporters live on the set of the newscast to introduce and close their stories.

We were asked to invite newsmakers to be live guests on the news so the anchorpeople could question them. Film was on its way out and the high tech mini cam was now the thing. We were doing more and more live reports from the field. It didn't matter if a story had happened earlier in the day; the reporter had to be "live" on the scene at news time even if it was dark out. I think, to this day, television would rather see Joe Trenchcoat or Mary Breathless live in the field rather than some actual news footage.

All of this attention on the television reporter gave us mini celebrity status. I was surprised to find myself being recognized on elevators. No longer were we the faceless narrators of news film. New York consultants were being brought in to teach us how to speak properly and how to walk, talk and gesture in front of the camera. A news director told me to get involved in the story, to really feel it. For the past fifteen years, I had been taught to play it straight as a reporter. I didn't like a lot of the changes.

Around this time a Florida-based supermarket tabloid newspaper assigned one of its reporters to sift through the garbage of former Secretary of State Henry Kissinger. Some documents were found, nothing earthshaking, but enough to make a splashy story for the supermarket news racks. For some reason this titillated someone in our news management and I heard some reporters were being asked to check the garbage cans behind the home of Mayor Richard J. Daley. They might have thought better after some reporters turned them down. I don't think the Daley garbage assignment ever took place.

One morning I'm sipping my coffee and reading the newspapers, and I notice our news director, the assignment editor and a couple of producers huddled in the middle of the newsroom. It has a conspiratorial look about it. I have just read an item that Mayor Bilandic's wife, Heather, has suffered a miscarriage. She is OK and resting at home. I become more suspicious of the pow-wow going on with my bosses because I see where they have called over our medical reporter for a conference. It isn't long before they want me, and the conversation goes something like this:

"Mrs. Bilandic has had a miscarriage and we want you to go out to the home to see if you can get reaction from the mayor."

"You mean you want me to ask the mayor how he feels about his wife's miscarriage?"

"Yes, maybe he'll hold a news conference."

I continue my protest. "Look, a miscarriage can happen in any family. It's a tragedy. But it's a private thing. Yes, it's the family of the mayor of Chicago and should be reported. But you don't need reaction."

"OK, you've made your point. Just go out there and let us know if there are any other camera crews there. Just protect us in case the mayor comes out to talk."

So we go out to the Bridgeport neighborhood and take a ride down Bilandic's block, past his house. There is absolutely nothing going on and I radio that to the desk. They call back asking us to stake it out for a little while just in case. We park down the street. Within a few minutes I see a policeman, Mike Graney, one of the mayor's detail, come out of the house and get into an unmarked car. He throws it in reverse and comes roaring back to where we're parked.

"Pete, what is it? What do you guys want?"

"Our desk wanted us to see if the mayor is going to comment on his wife."

"Aw, Pete, this is a private family matter. He's not going to say anything. He just wants to be alone with his wife."

"You're right. We're gonna get out of here."

We take off and I radio the desk. I'm angry and embarrassed and I tell them I'm leaving.

The desk man gets his back up.

"You mean you're refusing the assignment?"

"Yes," I reply.

I think I might get fired but when I return, nothing is said. No one pushes it any further. I go on to the next assignment. But that was the level we were reaching in television news.

Later on, late in both their lives, the Bilandics did become parents. A son was born, Michael Morgan Bilandic. He would be a great source of joy for the rest of their days. That was news.

On February 4, 1977, Mayor Bilandic would be at the scene of one of the city's worst mass transit disasters. During the evening rush hour, a train rider's worst nightmare occurred. As an El train rounded the curve at Lake Avenue and Wabash Street it plowed into another stopped train, causing cars to go off the tracks and topple to the street below. Twelve people were killed and at least 180 were injured. Bilandic, whose office was several blocks away, went to the scene to help coordinate city services. He watched as John Cardinal Cody and ministers of all denominations prayed with the dying.

Early in 1978, the Bilandic administration faced a real scandal. A team of *Chicago Sun Times* reporters and investigators from the Better Government Association opened a small tavern on North Wells Street called the Mirage. Their mission: to see firsthand if city inspectors were on the take. It wasn't long before the inspectors showed up and performed according to billing. In return for cash, they were quite willing to overlook violations of the plumbing and electrical codes and ignore obvious health and fire hazards in the building. The story got national attention on *Sixty Minutes*. The Bilandic administration responded with the creation of an Office of Professional Review to uncover corruption at City Hall. Three building inspectors and a fire inspector were suspended and investigations were launched.

The winter of 1978 wasn't going so well. Heavy snow and cold snarled the city. The salt supply dwindled to 2500 tons. The city had to resort to use of sand, a process that had a side effect of clogging the sewers, according to the Streets and Sanitation Department. Twenty-seven hundred miles of side streets were jammed. Plows had to be put on garbage trucks. Eighteen hundred city workers were put on the street with shovels to clear the way to bus stops. Winds blew windows out of high rise buildings. Thirty thousand Chicagoans would be unable to pay their utility bills. It would be much worse the next year.

Other problems faced the Bilandic administration. Policemen and firemen were clamoring for collective bargaining agreements. Bilandic was opposed. He wanted to maintain Mayor Daley's old policy of a handshake deal. Some of the newer and younger aldermen were restless. They wanted pay raises and more respect from Tom Donovan and the department heads. Calling themselves the "reluctant rebels," they let it be known that the iron rule of the Daley era wouldn't cut it under the new Bilandic administration.

In February, President Jimmy Carter came to town. He was a new kind of president who promised not to lie to the American people who were weary from the Watergate scandal. Mr. Carter was often photographed getting off an airplane carrying his own garment bag and wearing that famous grin. In keeping with his humble and frugal ways, the president would stay in private homes while traveling. During this trip to Chicago, the president stayed at the home of Heather and Mike Bilandic on South Union Avenue. I was assigned to cover this event and stood on the street in front of the home amidst a growing crowd of curious Bridgeporters. The newlywed couple had been to French cooking class and was serving the president duck l'orange and chocolate mousse. A young bystander proudly recalled how he had once hunted chocolate mousse in Canada.

On March 4, the *Chicago Daily News* printed its last edition and closed its doors for good. There wasn't anything Bilandic or anyone else could do. The 102-year-old Chicago institution had won thirteen Pulitzer Prizes and was renowned for its foreign coverage and, of course, the Pulitzer Prize-winning columnist Mike Royko. Royko and some of the other stars of the paper would go to the *Sun Times* and the *Tribune.* Many others would be out of work. One reporter described the scene in the city room like a last day of school, people cleaning out their desks and autographing books about the *Daily News*. The usual newspaper wake was held later at the Billy Goat Tavern.

Later that month, on St. Patrick's Day, Jane Byrne and Jay McMullen were married at Queen of All Saints Basilica in the Sauganash neighborhood where Jane had grown up. With the closing of the *Daily News,* Jay joined his new wife in the ranks of the unemployed. Within a short time, Jane Byrne would announce her candidacy for the Democratic nomination for mayor of Chicago. No one paid much attention.

In the summer of 1978, the Bilandic administration inaugurated ChicagoFest, a music and food extravaganza at the old Navy Pier on the lakefront. Copied after a summer festival in Milwaukee, the mayor and his wife Heather would dutifully appear at ChicagoFest every day.[1]

New Year's Eve 1978 is a Saturday and sometime during the morning hours it begins to snow in Chicago. At first it's very pretty. The snow continues to fall all day and into the evening. It gets deeper and deeper. It reminds me of my boyhood in Buffalo, New York. It's fun at first. We go out with the kids and play in the yard. We come in and warm up. And still the snow keeps coming. It is still snowing at nightfall.

My wife and I are scheduled to go to a New Year's Eve party less than two miles from home. But that is soon out of the question. You can't even walk in it. And it is kind of fun really, to hunker down with the kids in front of the TV. And it keeps snowing. And when we get up the next morning, it is an incredible sight.

Most people probably never see this much snow at one time in their lifetime. It is gorgeous. The trees are covered. And, as I say, it is fun at first. Then Monday morning comes and everyone has to try to get to work.

I take the train downtown and walk through paths in the snow to the Merchandise Mart. For our newsroom, the blizzard is the only story for the next couple of months.

---

1   Davis, "Running Chicago".

When the snow finally stops on New Year's Day, the bitter cold moves into Chicago and the temperatures plummet. It's a struggle just to walk to a train or a bus. Few people can get to their cars. I go out with a crew to record some of these scenes. Plows cannot get to the side streets and they are a total disaster. Cars are strewn everywhere. Some hardy souls are able to dig their cars out and begin a Chicago tradition of placing a chair in the street to save their parking space. There are few violations of this system.

On Friday night, January 12, it starts snowing again and doesn't stop until Sunday morning, leaving a record-breaking twenty-seven inches of snow on the ground. For the city of Chicago, coping with the snow and the cold together is next to impossible. It is misery for the next two months. The new administration of Michael Bilandic would commit several errors that only made things worse.

Being on the streets this winter in Chicago is like being in a different world. One night I find myself out on the South Side. There's a report that a specialized team of snow fighters with thirty-four pieces of equipment is on the way from Buffalo, New York, snow capital of the world. But the city is being very secretive about it. This surprises me because I think this would be some good news for a change. Just by luck I find one of the plows. It's from a company called Sno-Go. A young man steps down from his truck to be interviewed. His truck is equipped with a humongous snow blower device on the front, the likes of which I have never seen before. He is a pleasant fellow who knows some people back in Buffalo I know. His name rings a bell with me. Is he an outfit guy? That's not important now. He's got this fantastic plow and he's clearing the streets and it makes for a good story. Months later there would be a report in the newspaper that some hoods from Buffalo had ripped off Chicago while leasing the city snow plows during the blizzard of '79.

Bilandic appeared on TV with his top aides, all wearing turtleneck sweaters, but everything was going downhill fast. The Chicago Transit Authority was a mess. Train service was disrupted. People were left waiting in the freezing cold at train stations. There are vivid television pictures of empty El trains going through stops in predominantly black neighborhoods on the South Side, as crowds of chilled passengers looked on in disgust. To this day, African Americans believe Bilandic ordered the trains not to stop so they could service white neighborhoods to the north. "It was a personal insult," said community activist Nancy Jefferson. "Jane Byrne picked up strong support in the black wards after that."[2]

Someone in the Bilandic administration came up with a bright idea. The city would plow school parking lots so residents could dig out their cars and park them there temporarily. Addresses of the lots to be plowed were published in the *Tribune*. People worked all day to extricate their cars from the side streets. But when they reached the closest parking lot, it was covered with snow. The city had issued the wrong list. The longtime head of the city's snow command, Emmett Garrity, was fired.

Then, as a final touch, there was a rally of precinct captains at the Bismarck Hotel right before the election. It was a traditional affair like a high school pep rally. There were many speeches praising the Bilandic administration and its "herculean efforts" during this terrible storm. The speeches droned on. Most of the reporters left. One who didn't was Bill Griffin of the *Tribune*. Bilandic finally got up and likened himself to Christ crucified. "In the early history of Christianity, you see a leader, starting with twelve disciples. They crucify the leader and make martyrs of the others. And what was the result? Christianity is bigger and stronger than it was before. It's our turn to be in the trenches to see if we are made of the same stuff as the early Christians, the millions of Jews persecuted by the Nazis, oppressed Polish people and enslaved blacks in America." Griffin couldn't believe his ears. It was the headline story in the paper the next morning.

Michael Bilandic wasn't the only politician frustrated during this election cycle. Consider a young man named John McCaffrey who was running as the Democratic organization candidate in the 44thWard. The 44thWard then and today can be described as trendy, politically independent, politically correct and upscale. It also was the heart of the city's gay community. Because of his independent

---

2   "Eyes on the Prize," *PBS*.

electorate, McCaffrey sometimes had to take potshots at his friends in City Hall so he would not sound like a party hack. McCaffrey opened his campaign office on Southport Avenue and soon found out he was just a few doors from a house of ill repute. It was a place called Queens and Kings, which offered nude wrestling with the lady of your choice. Even though he tried to get the place closed, his opponents circulated fliers in the neighborhood saying McCaffrey was for prostitution. When the gay candidate dropped out of the race and threw his support to McCaffrey, opponents passed out fliers at Sunday masses showing a picture of him with the gay candidate and saying McCaffrey was also pro-abortion. Add to that that he was the candidate supported by an administration that couldn't seem to get rid of the snow. It was his first try for public office and John McCaffrey just couldn't seem to catch a break. He lost.

For the mayor, the bad news wouldn't stop. His elderly and beloved mother, Minnie Bilandic, the woman who told him never to stand in the way of a draft, passed away.

One week before the election, a Democratic Party poll had Bilandic and Byrne in a dead heat. A Channel 7 (ABC) poll had Bilandic in the lead 47% to 41%. A Channel 2 (CBS) poll had Byrne leading 50% to 38%.

There were no thawing temperatures until February 20, two days before the primary election. The day before the election the moon passed between the earth and the sun, causing a rare eclipse and casting a shadow across the city. On Election Day, the sun was shining brightly and you could actually see some snow melting. People came out to vent their anger.

It was the biggest defeat for the Democratic Machine of Chicago in nearly a half century. Illinois Governor James Thompson called it the biggest upset in the history of the state. All of the oranges lined up in a row for Jane Byrne, just like a Las Vegas slot machine.

There was a near-record turnout with 57% of the eligible voters going to the polls. Byrne won by 17,000 votes out of 800,000 cast.

Bilandic was out. Jane Byrne was no longer unemployed.

PART II

The Candidates

✳ CHAPTER 3 ✳

Jane M. Byrne

I HAVE THIS IMAGE *of Jane Byrne. She's out campaigning on Milwaukee Avenue near Division Street, the old Polish neighborhood just northwest of the Loop.*

She's walking along, trying to engage passersby. She has one aide trailing behind her. But it's cold and nobody wants to talk. They grab a piece of the literature, stuff it in their pocket, pull their coat tight at the neck and hustle away. Jane is in a cloth coat and wearing a blonde wig.

You have to understand there isn't anything wrong with her real hair. But it's the type that needs constant tending. And when you're running a bare budget campaign, well, there just isn't the time or the money to do the hair properly. So this goofy wig is her trademark during the campaign.

Now, I'm out there with a camera crew trying to cover this lackluster campaign event on Milwaukee Avenue and Jane, God bless her, is trying to make the best of it. She's smiling and bubbly. And, when I put her on camera, she's just as enthusiastic and confident about winning. But I'm thinking we both know at this point in time the campaign is going nowhere. She's been fired from her job at City Hall. She's bucking the powerful Democratic Machine. There's no money and few prospects because everyone thinks she's a loser. Even our coverage is perfunctory. An assignment editor had said, "Whatever happened to Jane Byrne? Isn't she still running for mayor?" So that's the only reason we're out there. It's a cold, gray winter day in Chicago, December 1978, before the snows came.

45

The dean of independent politics in Chicago is Don Rose. His involvement began while he was still in high school in the late 1940s but he blossomed in the 1960s as an activist in the civil rights movement. He was the press secretary for Dr. Martin Luther King, Jr., when the civil rights leader brought his crusade to Chicago and was stymied by Mayor Richard J. Daley's Democratic Machine.

Daley was able to spar with Dr. King because there were many blacks in his organization who held jobs and political office. Daley prevailed on them to form a committee in support of his policies and opposing the tactics of Dr. King. One of them was Harold Washington. Don Rose and others remember how he hated that role and how Harold was the only organization man who came to parties and other gatherings held by Dr. King's followers.

A student of ward politics throughout the city, Rose was successful in helping many black independents get elected on the South Side in the late 1960s. He also helped William Singer win a special election for alderman in what was then the 44th Ward on the North Side. This was the same William Singer who, along with Rev. Jesse Jackson, ousted the late Mayor Daley's delegation to the 1972 Democratic National Convention.

Don Rose also managed Harold Washington's unsuccessful bid for mayor against Michael Bilandic in 1977. It was only a matter of time before he would hook up with Jane Byrne, who was seeking the Machine's grand prize. Rose was also a freelance writer who wrote a dining column for the *Chicago Sun Times,* where he got to know Jay McMullen, City Hall reporter for the other Field Enterprises paper, the *Daily News.* McMullen, who was close to Byrne, asked him to help and Don Rose signed on. When he came aboard, there wasn't much to the Byrne campaign. They had an office in the old Monadnock Building on West Jackson. The office space was provided by Byrne's brother, attorney Edward Burke, not to be confused with Alderman Ed Burke.

It was fall and there wasn't a hint of snow in the air and Jane Byrne looked like another entry in the record book of also rans against the Machine. Yet everybody was upbeat, including the candidate. Rose developed a strategy and wrote some speeches. Although he said he never had a title, he was acting like a campaign manager. Rose said Jane Byrne was the best candidate he ever worked with. She listened. She took direction. She began wearing suits and a wig to control her noisy hair. Andy Bajonski, who had worked on former Governor Dan Walker's successful campaign against the party in the 1972 primary election, was the press secretary.

Rose told Edward Burke they would need $75,000 to run a credible radio and TV campaign for the last few weeks before the election. Somehow Burke raised the money and Rose made the commercials. He had obtained a tape of the late Mayor Daley saying beautiful things about Jane Byrne. It was incorporated into both radio and TV. Then there was the famous commercial with Byrne standing out in the snow.

When the storms hit, Rose remembered Byrne leading marches down the subway platform in the Loop from Jackson Boulevard to Lake Street. She was cheered by the most angry transit riders and you could feel something happening. "I won't let you down," Jane Byrne told the crowds. On election night she proclaimed, "I'm going to run it straight and I'm going to run it clean. There will be no clout and the fifty wards in the city will share the work of the city."[1]

After Byrne's victory in the primary election, things slowly began to change. Rose made some public statements that angered her. A reporter asked him if he was going to be the city's new patronage chief. Rose answered that it would be interesting to preside over the butcher shop but he didn't want that job. He busied himself trying to line up a City Council majority for Byrne with the idea of demoting what Byrne called the "evil cabal" of men there. At the top of the list were Aldermen Edward Vrdolyak of the 10th Ward and Edward Burke of the 14th.

But Byrne was being wooed intensely by the regular Democrats. She had talked with Party Chairman George Dunne. Senator Rich Daley and former Lieutenant Governor Neil Hartigan were calling. So was Vrdolyak. Charlie Swibel, a slick real estate mogul and head of the Chicago Housing Authority, was sending flowers. There was

---

1 *Chicago Tribune,* February 27, 1979.

talk that Byrne needed to make peace with the Party regulars or they might try to defeat her in the general election. Some of the regulars were also approaching her husband, Jay McMullen. Jane Byrne had begun the transition back to the Party from whence she had come.

On April 3, 1979, Chicagoans came out in record numbers to elect Jane Byrne as one of the first woman mayors of any large city in the United States. The Democratic Party was operating full blast for her.

Don Rose was anathema to the Democratic organization. Although he was called occasionally for advice, as far as Jane Byrne was concerned, he was history.

Jane Byrne's first year as mayor was a wild roller coaster ride for Chicago. The news media loved it. The new mayor would often make important announcements as she walked down the corridors of City Hall. Her appointment of a new police superintendent was a process that went on for months. One day the new mayor saw Hugh Hill, the veteran Channel 7 political reporter, outside her office. Her aides winced as she whispered loudly to Hill, "It's Joe D. It's going to be Joe D." She was referring to Joseph DiLeonardi, a popular homicide detective who was in line for the top police job. Hill dutifully called his office to report he had the scoop of the day. When City Hall reporters followed up later, Byrne said that it might not be Joe D after all. But that's just the way she was. She couldn't restrain herself. It was all very refreshing in the beginning.

Byrne faced serious financial problems as she assumed office. The national economy was in shambles. Jimmy Carter was nearing the end of his first term as president. There was double digit inflation, gasoline shortages and a 15% prime interest rate. Unemployment was high. To use the president's own words, a "malaise" had fallen across the land. A series of horrible winters had stretched Chicago's budget thin. The school board was hundreds of millions of dollars in debt. There were no available loans and payrolls could not be met. School Superintendent Joseph Hannon abruptly resigned and left town.

Within two months, the city was forced to borrow $64 million to meet cash flow shortages. Byrne didn't help matters when she authorized a $70,000 remodeling project for her office, 15% pay raises for top city executives, and a tripling of her public relations staff.

The new mayor quickly let it be known that it would not be business as usual.

She said there were many loafers on the city payroll and began firing some of them. She dumped several ward superintendents and suspended others. The ward superintendent was responsible for all city services in a ward, such as garbage pick up, snow removal and tree trimming. These positions were held by men who were high up in the Democratic Party organization. But this did not faze Byrne. Among those she fired was a ward committeeman. Another was a state representative. A *Tribune* editorial praised her for attempting to eliminate waste and improve services. Many of those she fired were from the 11th Ward of Senator Richard M. Daley, the late mayor's son. All of a sudden, Daley and his allies were on her persona non grata list. Byrne got into a tiff with Michael Madigan, a powerful Democratic leader in the Illinois House and committeeman of the 13th Ward on the South Side. She accused Madigan of sitting on his hands when she wanted some legislation passed. She got his attention by firing one of his top ward lieutenants, Michael Cardilli, who held the number two spot in the Department of Streets and Sanitation. Madigan got the message and became a loyal follower. Two years later, Byrne would appoint Cardilli executive director of the Chicago Transit Authority, although he had no experience in mass transit.

Byrne added a touch of glamour and style to the mayor's office. She liked to travel and visited London and Ireland during her first year. There were impromptu vacations at the Palm Springs Tennis Club, owned by Chicago developer Harry Chaddick, a close friend of husband Jay McMullen. She took time off to have some cosmetic surgery. In August of her first year, she led a contingent of thirty city officials to Europe. They visited Rome, Paris and Nice.

That first summer, Byrne tried to cancel ChicagoFest, the summer event at Navy Pier started by Bilandic. The papers called it petty and the mayor had to reverse herself after a public outcry to keep the event going. To her credit, she expanded the idea and later came up with Taste of Chicago, Blues Fest, Gospel Fest, Jazz Fest and a series of ethnic neighborhood celebrations that are all still popular today. Along with the redevelopment of Navy Pier, these events are considered some of Byrne's major achievements in boosting Chicago tourism.

Shortly after her election, Byrne called *Tribune* reporter William Griffin and offered him a job. Griffin was a bit leery of her because of the way the taxi cab story unfolded. But he decided a career change might be good. He signed on as press secretary.

Probably because of her husband, Jane Byrne had an affinity for newspaper reporters. Paul McGrath, a *Sun Times* writer who had befriended her during the early days of the campaign, was appointed chief of staff. Like most journalists, McGrath was idealistic. Things began piling up on his desk as he tried to make sure all was on the up and up. As Byrne became closer to the regular Democrats, it was obvious McGrath's system wouldn't work. He was shuffled off to a fellowship at Harvard's Kennedy School of Government.

Bill Griffin replaced McGrath as chief of staff. Mike Brady, a state representative who couldn't get along with his ward committeeman, became the head of intergovernmental affairs, in charge of lobbying and patronage. Steve Brown, a young reporter who covered the legislature for the *Daily Herald,* was hired as Brady's assistant. During the early days of her administration, Brady and Griffin would be key advisors to Jane Byrne.

A major item on Jane Byrne's agenda was to appoint a new superintendent of police. During the campaign she had promised to fire Bilandic's chief of police, James O'Grady. O'Grady came in with his resignation early in the administration, and an African American by the name of Sam Nolan was appointed acting superintendent. Then a search began for a permanent replacement.

Bill Griffin, the chief of staff to the mayor, made what he believes was the worst decision of his brief career in city government. He recommended Joseph DiLeonardi to be Chicago's top cop.

DiLeonardi, or Joe D as he was known on the street, was the chief of homicide detectives. He looked like he came out of central casting. He was tall and had a hawk-like face and his suits were the best in the police department. They said that Joe D was the model for a popular television detective, Kojak, played by Telly Savalas. He was also liked by police reporters who appreciated his willingness to talk and his colorful quotes. Despite all the hoopla, Joe D had a reputation as a tough but honest cop. Bill Griffin knew him from his days as a police reporter for the City News Bureau.

When Byrne appointed DiLeonardi acting superintendent, she described him as a man of action who might be the permanent police chief she had been looking for. Joe D took immediate steps to crack down on Chicago's crime syndicate. He appointed William Duffy, an expert on organized crime, to be the deputy superintendent for inspectional services. A no-nonsense cop's cop, Duffy had been relieved of similar duties more than a decade earlier amid reports he would not be influenced by politicians and some of their hood friends. The appointment of Duffy was seen as a message to the crime syndicate from the Byrne administration that there would be no more business as usual.

Duffy replaced Deputy Superintendent William Hanhardt, who was long rumored to have crime syndicate connections. Nothing ever came of the rumors and Hanhardt later retired after thirty-three years of service. But many years later in 2001, at the age of 72, Hanhardt pleaded guilty to masterminding a series of mob-sponsored jewelry thefts in seven states that netted close to $5 million. As part of his plea agreement, Hanhardt agreed to pay $4.8 million in restitution. Only in Chicago.

Over the years, organized crime in Chicago has been well represented not only in the police department but also in local and state government. The center of this political operation has been the 1st Ward which, in my time, included the downtown "Loop" area and extended into some nearby Italian neighborhoods. After all, "outfit" guys are citizens, too, and many times have an interest in what government is doing to or for them.

The longtime alderman of the 1st Ward was Fred Roti. Roti was a little man with pleasant features and an engaging personality. Before coming to the City Council, he had served in the state legislature. He was a very knowledgeable legislator. On many occasions he would come to the City Hall press room to have coffee and cigarettes and to banter with reporters. He took a lot of ribbing about being the mob alderman and he took it good naturedly. During one Council election, a reporter came up with a great bumper sticker slogan for Alderman Roti: "Vote for Roti and nobody gets hurt." Roti roared with approval.

When Duffy took over the units that kept an eye on organized crime, some of the 1st Ward officials noticed something unusual. They were being followed by plain clothes policemen. Alderman Roti and other 1st Warders complained to City Hall. Their homes were being watched. They had police tails. What was it all about?

There were some other problems with DiLeonardi. He was more of a street cop and didn't take well to the administrative aspects of the job. But more importantly, he seemed to be getting more press than the mayor. And then there was the New Year's Eve celebration the mayor attended on State Street. When the crowd got unruly, Byrne turned to Acting Superintendent DiLeonardi and asked him to do something. He didn't act quickly enough, she later told her aides. He froze. He wasn't the man of action she thought he was. After that, Joe D was toast. She shut him out, refusing to take his phone calls. Soon DiLeonardi asked to have his name withdrawn from consideration for permanent status as superintendent of police. All he wanted was a job at O'Hare Airport, not far from his home. Both he and Duffy were demoted to the rank of captain.

But Joe D did not go quietly. He went to *Chicago Tribune* columnist Bob Wiedrich. He and Duffy accused the mayor's top aides of interfering with police work. DiLeonardi said Brady and Griffin told him to get rid of Duffy, that they were acting at the behest of 1st Ward Committeeman John D'Arco, a known associate of mob guys.

Bernard Carey, a Republican state's attorney, convened a grand jury. Mayor Byrne distanced herself from her two top aides. She told the *Tribune* she was clean. "Ask yourself," she said, "could Brady and Griffin have been acting without my knowledge?"

Brady and Griffin were flabbergasted. They had to hire attorneys. Mike Brady's father had been a policeman who was shot and killed in the line of duty. Griffin came from a family of honorable cops. Within a couple of days they tendered their resignations, claiming they had lost the confidence of the mayor. But they too had a couple of parting shots. They said their conversation with DiLeonardi regarding the removal of Duffy was grossly misunderstood. Brady quoted Joe D as telling him, "Mike, you wouldn't believe the things I could tell you I was asked to do by the mayor. I could blow the lid off." Nothing came of the grand jury investigation. Brady and Griffin went into private business and never returned to government.

There was one funny incident after the Brady-Griffin affair. For obvious reasons, Griffin had his home phone changed to an unlisted number. The phone company assigned his old number to a young bachelor named Mike Martin who had just moved into a basement apartment on the Northwest Side. His phone started ringing immediately. The crazy thing about it was that Martin sounded a lot like Griffin on the phone. At first Martin was annoyed, but when he found out who Griffin was, he began to enjoy his newfound fame. Reporters would call and Martin would scream, "No comment!" and hang up. One night, Martin's father came over, had a few drinks, and did a tour of duty on the phone. He told callers stories about leprechauns. Then what was bound to happen happened. Mayor Byrne called. Martin said it took him five minutes to convince her he was not Griffin. "She kept telling me this thing would blow over," he said.

Joseph DiLeonardi continued with the police department until his retirement after 36 years. In 1994, he was appointed U.S. Marshal for the Northern District of Illinois. He still had that Hollywood flare and some of his admirers thought he was a model for the crusading marshal played by Tommy Lee Jones in the blockbuster movies "The Fugitive" and "U.S. Marshals."

Jane Byrne and her husband Jay McMullen are having coffee in their forty-fourth floor condominium overlooking Chicago's Gold

Coast. The apartment has exquisite views of the city, a great perch for a new mayor to oversee the territory she governs. Mayor Byrne is not too shy to pick up the phone and call her underlings if she spots a fire or anything else amiss.

On this particular weekend, the Chicago Marathon is being run and she notices traffic congestion on Michigan Avenue. She picks up the phone, calls 911 and tells the dispatcher that police should do something about the traffic problem. There is an ambulance jammed in the mess. Ten minutes later she calls again, and this time she tells the dispatcher who she is. Later, the mayor and her husband are picked up by the limo and police detail that squire her around town. They are going to the marathon finish line for closing ceremonies. Inside the limo, the police radio is on. The voice of an officer is on the air, saying there was a beef from the mayor earlier about traffic on Michigan Avenue but it had been straightened out. Then the officer says maybe the mayor should come out and direct traffic herself. To the dismay of her bodyguards, Mayor Byrne takes the microphone and goes on the citywide police band. "Who said that?" "I did," comes the bold reply.

The next day at a news conference, Police Superintendent DiLeonardi said they were trying to identify this policeman. The mayor said she only wanted to talk to him for a moment. But the cop was smart. He remained anonymous.

Early in 1980, Mayor Byrne appointed her husband, Jay McMullen, as her press secretary at a salary of one dollar per year. He quickly canceled her impromptu news conferences, saying all she was doing was thinking out loud and the press was abusing her largesse. McMullen had already threatened to punch one reporter in the nose. Then he went on Irv Kupcinet's television show and threatened more bloody noses. After the taping, the mayor breezed right by reporters and her husband held his own impromptu press conference. The media gobbled it up.

Then they got mad at the *Chicago Tribune*. McMullen said they would evict the paper's reporter, Bob Davis, from the City Hall press room. The media was poised when the day of departure arrived. But McMullen and the mayor backed down.

The new mayor of Chicago dove headfirst into the national political arena. Jimmy Carter had a rough first term and Senator Edward Kennedy of Massachusetts was challenging his reelection bid. Byrne organized a major fundraising dinner at McCormick Place and invited the president. Ten thousand Democrats crowded the convention hall. The massive dais was a replica of the Delta Queen river boat, which the Carters had recently vacationed aboard. The night of the dinner, she told her audience and a beaming Jimmy Carter that if the convention were that night, she would vote in the party caucus to nominate the current leader for reelection.

Within two weeks, Mayor Byrne endorsed Teddy Kennedy for president. Byrne said later that her remarks at McCormick Place were not a real endorsement, that it was conditional. Carter and his people saw it differently.

Rev. James Wall, an ordained minister and editor of the *Christian Century* magazine, returned from a visit to the White House in October. Wall, who had run Carter's Illinois campaign in 1976, quoted high White House sources as saying Mayor Byrne had pledged her support to the president without any qualifications during Carter's visit to Chicago. Chicago pols thought it was a shrewd political move on Byrne's part, switching to Teddy. Kennedy was ahead in the polls. But that was about to change.

Early in November, CBS broadcast a documentary called "Teddy" which closely examined Senator Kennedy, his personality and his candidacy for president. According to overnight ratings services, the program attracted only a minor share of the audience in Chicago. The lion's share went to the blockbuster movie "Jaws" on another channel.

This was a break for Kennedy because the CBS program devastated him. Correspondent Roger Mudd threw Kennedy some tough questions about Chappaquiddick. The senator looked confused almost to the point of double talk. He appeared bewildered when asked basic questions as to why he wanted to be president and how he differed from President Carter.

At the same time, some Democratic ward committeemen in Chicago were discovering serious opposition to Kennedy in their neighborhoods, especially from women still angry about Chappaquiddick and the senator's widely publicized marital problems.

In July of 1969, Senator Kennedy attended a party on Chappaquiddick Island, off the coast of Massachusetts, in honor of several young women who had worked on his brother Bobby's presidential campaign before he was assassinated the year before. Ted Kennedy and twenty-eight-year-old Mary Jo Kopechne left the party together. Kennedy made a wrong turn and drove off a bridge into a pond. Kennedy escaped the sunken automobile and swam to safety while Ms. Kopechne drowned. The accident wasn't reported until the next day. Then there was a swift resolution of the case in local courts. The senator was convicted of leaving the scene of an accident, received a suspended sentence and temporarily lost his driving privileges. Volumes have been written about this incident, which many believe killed Kennedy's chances for the presidency.

Still, the Cook County Democratic Committee, at the behest of Mayor Byrne, went ahead and endorsed Kennedy for president in the Illinois primary election scheduled for March. Some of the committeemen admitted they were watching "Jaws" when Kennedy was on TV.

After Byrne endorsed Teddy Kennedy for president and influenced his endorsement by the Cook County Democratic Party, a man named Ed Quigley appeared at the office of Bill Griffin, who at the time was still chief of staff. Byrne had put the word out that she was going to hold a fundraiser for Kennedy.

"Big Ed", as Quigley was known, was an old war horse of the Party. He was the city's sewer commissioner and also the committeeman of the 27th Ward on the West Side. Quigley doubled as a sergeant-at-arms for the Cook County Democratic Central Committee meetings. "Bouncer" would have been a more accurate title because of Quigley's strong shoving and elbowing abilities and his talent for fast ejection of any unwanted persons at the meetings.

On this day, Quigley arrived with a large box which he threw on Griffin's desk. "What's this?" Griffin asked. "It's for Kennedy," replied Quigley. The box was full of cash, wads of bills bound with rubber bands. Griffin told Quigley he couldn't take it. He said he needed checks and names and addresses of the donors. Quigley was angered. He took the box and left, muttering something about they never did business that way when the old man was alive. "The old man isn't here," Griffin said.

The afternoon of the 1980 Illinois primary election, Griffin received a phone call from Big Ed.

"What do you need?"

"What do you mean what do I need?"

"For Kennedy."

"We want him to win."

"C'mon, c'mon, I need a number."

"I don't have a number."

Then there was the St. Patrick's Day Parade issue. The mayor's press secretary husband, the always subtle Jay McMullen, told one reporter that President Carter could not march in Chicago's St. Patrick's Day Parade because he wasn't Irish. He called the president a Georgia cracker. That remark sent some shockwaves through the Peach state. Georgia state Senator Paul Broun was so insulted he introduced a resolution of protest in the Georgia legislature. When asked by a reporter how the people of Georgia felt about Mayor Byrne, Broun replied, "I couldn't tell you over the phone; it would burn up the wire." Carter didn't come.

But Senator Kennedy did march in the parade at the mayor's invitation. Afterward, he might have wished there had been an important vote in the senate. First of all, the weather was terrible. Wet rain had turned into huge hunks of sleet. Kennedy was late. There was a lot of booing as the senator greeted Mayor Byrne when the parade stepped off. Kennedy, suspecting the boos were for Byrne, quickly dropped back from the mayor's entourage. But Kennedy and his family encountered their own boos. In those days, many of the spectators along the route were roaring drunk. The Kennedys had to endure shouts of, "What about Chappaquiddick? Where's Mary Jo?" The Illinois primary election was held the next day. Kennedy was defeated by President Jimmy Carter. Mayor Byrne's handpicked candidate in the race for state's attorney, Alderman Eddie Burke, was soundly beaten by state Senator Richard M. Daley.

Jane Byrne's first year as mayor wasn't going so well. Her bal-lyhooed plan to revitalize the city's neighborhoods hadn't been unveiled. There were reports that the new budget would increase sewer taxes and auto license fees. She helped get Cook County a penny increase in the sales tax and used her power to stop signifi-cant sales tax relief in the legislature. Then, right before Christmas, employees of the Chicago Transit Authority went on strike.

One of my news commentaries from this period depicts a fictional Chicago housewife writing home to her mother downstate. Dear Mom, The CTA went on strike this morning. Herman walked ten blocks to the Northwestern Station but boarded on the wrong side of the tracks and ended up in Evanston. He took a cab back to the Loop for twenty dollars. I drove our car to the gas station but the lines were so long I came back home. Junior is still in school but that could end any day because the Board of Education is broke. We're expecting a nice hike in our property taxes soon to bail out the schools. You've probably read about the rape epidemic here. I heard a radio commercial from a guy named Eddie Burke who's running for state's attorney. It told how I could get a free rape alert whistle. But when I called the number it was temporarily discon-nected. Our neighbor, Mrs. Dombrowski, said none of this would have happened if Mayor Daley were still alive. Love from your struggling daughter in Chicago. P.S. Smoke detectors might be very good gifts for Christmas because we're afraid the firemen will go on strike any day now.

But the mayor was widely praised for her handling of the Chicago Transit Authority strike. She had appointed a former state repre-sentative, Eugene Barnes, to head the CTA. Barnes had once been a bus driver and he was a smart manager. The second day of the strike, the CTA was able to get a limited train schedule going by using supervisory personnel. Riders weren't charged for the service because the CTA was saving lots of money due to the work stop-page. It was a great public relations move. Byrne was given high marks for not caving into the unions. The strike was over in four days. The worst labor troubles were yet to come.

The schools were still a financial mess. The projected shortfall for the 1980 fiscal year was close to $500 million. Byrne blamed Governor Thompson and said it was the responsibility of the state of Illinois to fund public schools. The chairman of the new financial oversight committee for the schools, Jerome Van Gorkom, said, "The situation is not serious. It is desperate."

Early in 1980, Governor Thompson held a series of summit meetings in the state capitol at Springfield to address the Chicago school crisis. A complex financial rescue plan was worked out, which included money from the state of Illinois, the city of Chicago and heavy borrowing from nervous banks. But the money was slow in coming. The school board was unable to pay teachers and other union employees. There was no pay for the Christmas recess. The Teachers Union threatened to close the schools if they were not paid. There was considerable acrimony between the mayor and the president of the Teachers Union, Robert Healey. It played out on TV every night. The crisis dragged on through the month of January. Finally the teachers refused to work and for all practical purposes the schools were closed. The school board said the schools would remain open, but even Mayor Byrne said she wouldn't send her child to school if there were no teachers on duty. The schools were closed for two weeks. Byrne conducted marathon negotiations and a settlement was finally reached.

On February 14, 1980, during the darkness of night and without any immediate announcement, Chicago's firemen went on strike. They had been threatening to do so for months. Picket lines were set up at all the fire stations. An estimated 90% of the firemen honored the picket lines. More than half of the fire stations were shut down. Byrne, who had promised the firemen a contract during her campaign, now rejected their demands for increased fire truck crews, the inclusion of supervisors in the union, and the right to strike in the future.

To her credit, Mayor Byrne had a contingency plan. More than six hundred new recruits were signed up for duty. After two days of training they were used to haul hoses while supervisors and non-strikers went into the burning buildings. Workers from other departments were called in to help in emergencies. Police performed extra duties at fire scenes. There were no major disasters, but people did die. A two-year-old girl and her one-year-old brother were killed in a fire and an explosion at their home, one half-block from a closed fire station. The mayor and the hard-charging president of the Firefighter's Union, Frank "Moon" Muscare, traded insults on television.

The strike is two weeks old and I'm out on the picket line one night with the firemen. It's hard not to have some sympathy for these guys. One man is very depressed because his close friend has stopped striking and returned to work. "I saw him coming back from a fire," he said, "His face was covered with dirt. He had his hat and boots on. I felt real bad. I wanted to be with him." Another picket suggests to me that firemen as a group aren't very smart. "We don't know much about handling the public relations of this thing. It's all new to us. We're alone in this, but we're not going to give up." A policeman has this comment: "What can I tell you about these guys. They're not like cops. They like to go into burning buildings and breathe smoke. They may not be too smart, but they're all heart and guts."

The strike had its zany moments. A battalion chief drove a fire truck up to City Hall. He was protesting any agreement that would give the strikers amnesty. A judge who was trying to mediate the dispute was accused of being in bed with labor by Mayor Byrne's press secretary husband, Jay McMullen. The judge threw union leader Moon Muscare in jail, calling him a liar and a bigmouth.

The strike was an agonizing and emotional ordeal for the firemen. Proud and dedicated firefighters broke down and cried inside and outside the firehouses. Families and lifetime friendships were torn apart. The men who remained on duty were physically exhausted and fearful of fighting fires with amateurs. Byrne's get-tough approach didn't seem to work. As one frustrated wife said, "She may have forgotten she's dealing with guys who come out of smoking buildings coughing up blood and whose eyelashes have frozen shut while manning hoses at twenty below. They want to go back to work but they won't go with their tails between their legs."

Byrne was unable to negotiate with union leaders. Then, with the mayor's blessing, Rev. Jesse Jackson stepped in and helped negotiate a settlement. The strike had lasted twenty-three days.

Jane Byrne had been in office less than a year. She had alienated thousands of firemen, transit workers, teachers and others, all of whom had relatives and friends. A *Chicago Tribune* poll showed that 43% of Chicagoans rated her performance as poor. Only 14% thought she was doing a good or excellent job.

Chicago Sun Times columnist Mike Royko, who had been elated when she defeated the Chicago Democratic Machine, began referring to Byrne as Mayor Bossy. The *Tribune's* political editor, F. Richard Ciccone, was writing about an inner struggle between "Good Jane" and "Bad Jane."

In Springfield, state Senator Harold Washington introduced a bill establishing a recall procedure for the mayor of Chicago. It fell only six votes short of passage. State Senator Jeremiah Joyce, an ally of Rich Daley, said he preferred a plan which would require the mayor to submit to a psychiatric exam if 20% of the voters petitioned for it. That brought a lot of laughs on the Senate floor, but Joyce said he was dead serious.

In her second year as mayor, Jane Byrne alienated another large segment of Chicago's population, the African American community. She appointed a brand new school board and added minority members. The board promptly elected Rev. Kenneth Smith, a black minister, as its new president. Byrne went ballistic because the board had not consulted her about this action. She threatened to replace the entire board, but cooler heads prevailed and talked her out of it.

In March of 1981, Mayor Jane Byrne had a brainstorm. One morning she heard on the radio that there had been another shooting at Cabrini Green, the crime-ridden public housing project less than a dozen blocks from her Gold Coast high rise. She could see the drab buildings from her apartment window. The mayor later toured the project and was angered and shaken when she encountered a young girl in the back of a police cruiser, curled up in the fetal position. Police said she had been gang raped. The mayor did some research and found there had been ten deaths and more than thirty shootings at the project in less than three months. Cabrini Green had been the setting for a popular television sitcom called "Good Times" about a single mom trying to raise her family in public housing. But television couldn't capture the horrible living conditions there, which included a daily diet of gang warfare, drugs, guns, sniper shootings and rape. People who grew up at Cabrini and survived remember never being allowed outside without a parent with them.

So Mayor Jane Byrne took her husband, Jay McMullen, and moved into a fourth floor apartment on Sedgewick Street. Her security detail took an apartment next door. The move attracted national media attention, including articles in the *New York Times* and *Time* Magazine.

Critics of the mayor's move called it a major publicity stunt, that she was trying to win back the black community which had been angered when she dumped two black members of the Board of Education and replaced them with two white people, one of whom had been a strong opponent of mandatory school desegregation. Marion Stamps, a Cabrini Green mother and activist, would later call Byrne's move an insult, the ultimate in disrespect.

But Renault Robinson, an African American member of the Housing Authority, thought Byrne had shown guts moving to Cabrini. Many Cabrini Green residents welcomed their new neighbor, knowing she would bring some security to the tormented buildings.

She brought more than that. "City government was falling all over itself to provide extra services to Cabrini," she would say later in her book, *My Chicago.* "The maintenance men on the CHA payroll were both embarrassed by the state of things and frightened they might get fired. I relied on the Departments of Sewers, Streets and Sanitation and Public Works to clean up the project. The Department of Human Services provided paint, and tenant volunteers gathered to paint over the graffiti. Consumer Affairs set up food co-ops so residents could buy cheaper in bulk."[2]

---

2 Jane Byrne, *My Chicago* (New York: W.W. Norton Co.; Evanston: Northwestern University Press, 1992), 320.

Byrne found living at Cabrini not uncomfortable, but a sobering experience. "The first night a group of elementary school youngsters came to my door. They wanted to know what it was like to be mayor and whether I'd be staying for awhile. (The answer was yes.) I invited the children to stop by every evening. Our talks would become a ritual. The next knock on the door that first night came from two teenage girls, Lilli and Tina. I invited them in to discuss my goals for Cabrini. They too visited every night."[3]

In her book, Byrne describes with relish her efforts to end the drug war between two gangs, the Disciples and the Stones, a main cause of the violence at Cabrini. Byrne believed that organized crime was the source of the drugs. So she called in the City Council's link to organized crime, 1st Ward Alderman Fred Roti. Byrne dropped a big hint for him to get the word around that anyone involved in drugs at Cabrini was in for trouble. Roti played dumb, said he didn't know anything about this stuff. Next, she put out a call for Anthony "Tony the Ant" Spilotro, the Chicago mob's man in Las Vegas. She actually reached Spilotro at a hotel in Palm Springs, California. Spilotro said he thought the mayor had "balls" moving into Cabrini Green, but he insisted he wasn't into drugs. Still Byrne threatened to turn Rush Street into an extension of Holy Name Cathedral if something wasn't done at Cabrini. Rush Street, the city's night club district, had long been a staging ground for organized crime activity. After three weeks, Byrne says the gangbangers were pleading for her to leave, promising to stop the violence. A few days later, the mayor and her husband moved back to their Gold Coast residence.[4]

Charles Swibel, a Byrne confidante and major fundraiser, finally resigned as chairman of the Chicago Housing Authority. The mayor replaced him with a white man, Andrew Mooney. Then she appointed two white women to the CHA board. Byrne said she learned from her stay at Cabrini that the projects are a matriarchal society and women were needed to oversee the CHA. The Housing

---

3 Jane Byrne, *My Chicago*, 329.
4 Ibid.

Authority, whose tenants were more than 80% African American, now had three whites and two blacks on its board. The black community was outraged.

After two years in office, Byrne claimed to have streamlined city government and put the city on a sound financial footing. To accomplish this, the taxpayers of Chicago had to endure $400 million in new or increased taxes and fees.

Shortly after the beginning of her term, Jane Byrne began a war with Senator Richard M. Daley, son of the late mayor. The mayor and her advisors believed young Daley was the main threat to her political future. There were mass firings of 11th Ward people who had dominated the city payroll. Some of them were later reinstated by court actions. But this did not deter the mayor. She was relentless. Most of the other aldermen, long weary of 11th Ward dominance, were delighted by the mayor's purge. Daley was out on his own. He had a handful of allies who stuck with him at their own peril.

Byrne went out of her way to punish Daley and his allies. Sometimes it got out of hand. A case in point was what appeared to be a routine transfer of two ward superintendents. Ed Walsh, who was the superintendent of the 19th Ward, was sent to the 50th Ward. Joe Meyers, who had been running things in the 50th, was sent to replace Walsh in the 19th. It didn't seem like a big deal, except that the 50th Ward is in the far northeast corner of the city and the 19th is in the far southwest corner, a distance of about thirty miles. And it's a nightmare of a drive because there are no easy expressway routes. The ward superintendents are on 24-hour call, especially in snow season. They supervise garbage pickup, street cleaning and pothole repair. Byrne's people denied the transfer had anything to do with Ed Walsh running as a Carter delegate to the Democratic Convention. Byrne had dropped Carter and switched to Kennedy. Walsh was also close to 19th Ward Committeeman Tom Hynes, who was tight with Daley and high up on the Byrne enemies list. Joe Meyers, who was commuting south, seemed to be the victim of a battle between his ward committeeman and alderman.

In her first term as mayor, Jane Byrne became one of the best political fundraisers in the city's history. In four years, according to reports by the Board of Elections, she raised nearly $11 million. From this war chest she spent freely, paying her husband, Jay McMullen, $343,700 in salaries. She was also generous, one year giving more than $100,000 to charitable causes. Jane Byrne would need a lot of money for her reelection campaign.

✸ CHAPTER 4 ✸

Harold Washington

HE WAS A BACHELOR most of his life and his apartment was a mess: clothes all over the place, books, magazines, old newspapers, position papers, mimeographed fliers from the neighborhood. His suits were rumpled and his ties were stained. For as long as anyone can remember, even back to his boyhood, he was reading all the time.

"I remember Harold Washington when he lived in an apartment over a liquor store at 47th and Cottage Grove. It was probably in the '50s. He had one room up there. I was playing piano at a place called Killer Johnson's Archway Lounge across the street and Harold came in all the time. I don't remember him as a big drinker in those days. He would sit in a back booth with Killer Johnson and sometimes the Jones brothers; the South Side policy kings would be there and they would talk politics. We liked it because they would give us tips for playing special requests. I later found out from people in the neighborhood that, if someone got in trouble, Harold would give them legal advice free of charge. Harold was an eloquent speaker and I remember George Dunne, the Democratic Party chairman, once told me that Harold was the smartest man who ever walked the floors of City Hall."[1] [Russ Ewing, jazz pianist who would later become one of Chicago's top television reporters.]

---

1   Russ Ewing, interviewed by author, Paw Paw, MI, September 25, 2007.

Harold must have sympathized with the Jones brothers. In later years, as a member of the Illinois legislature, he would sponsor legislation to make the policy game legal. It never got enough votes.

He was born in 1922 and grew up on the tough streets of Chicago's South Side black belt. Harold fared better than many of his contemporaries coming of age in the Great Depression. His father, Roy L. Washington, Sr., was a lawyer who became an assistant corporation counsel for the city of Chicago and a Democratic precinct captain, even though the black neighborhood in those days voted mostly Republican.

When he was only four years old, Harold's mother, Bertha, left the family and Roy Sr. was given custody of Harold, his older two brothers and a sister. The two oldest children, Roy Jr. and Elizabeth, were sent to live with grandparents. Harold and his brother Edward were enrolled in a boarding school for children of black professionals in Milwaukee. Bertha remained in the neighborhood and helped with the children even after she and Roy Sr. were divorced. Bertha would remarry and have six more children.

Harold was only four and a half years old and his brother six when they were shipped off to St. Benedict The Moor School in Milwaukee, Wisconsin, about 70 miles away. Neither would ever adapt to the strict environment of the school run by Capuchin priests. The Washington boys frequently ran away. After a few years, Roy Sr. relented and brought his sons back to Chicago and the local public schools.

Roy Sr. was an ordained minister in the African Methodist Episcopal Church. He preached at several different churches on the South Side. Sometimes he would take his son Harold to church with him and the boy would say a line or two to the congregation. He loved it. Later he would help his father with precinct work, passing out campaign literature. Prominent African American politicians of the day would come to the Washington home and young Harold was all ears.

Harold Washington seemed to have all the makings of a future leader. He was a star hurdler at DuSable High School. Yet there was a carelessness about him that would cause him problems for the rest of his life. He was stubborn and at times had a short fuse.

Classmates at DuSable recall the young, bookish Washington being forgetful, sometimes appearing at a track meet without his running shoes. He had a high end vocabulary and friends sometimes had to check the dictionary after a conversation with him. He was strong willed and helped organize students to persuade DuSable administrators to keep the gym and swimming pool open for longer hours.

Even though he was a good student, he quit school after three years, claiming the work didn't challenge him anymore. He joined the Civilian Conservation Corps, a Depression-era government work program. He would spend six months planting trees in Michigan and working in a limestone quarry. Returning home, he got a job at the Wilson Meat Packing House in the stockyards where his father had worked his way through law school. Later, with his father's clout and his own ability to pass a civil service exam, Harold would land a job as a clerk in the Chicago office of the U.S. Treasury Department.

By this time, the young Mr. Washington was in love. Her name was Nancy Dorothy Finch and she lived in the same apartment building. Roy Sr. married the couple in the living room of his home in the summer of 1941. She was seventeen and he was nineteen. The marriage would be brief and end in divorce. Years later, when Harold ran for mayor, reporters located the former Mrs. Washington in Tennessee. She had nothing but good things to say about Harold.

One reason for the short-lived marriage was World War II. Harold was drafted into the Army Air Corps and sent to the South Pacific where he worked as a soil technician constructing air strips. The U.S. Army was still a segregated institution. He became a first sergeant and earned a high school diploma. Many years later, when he had passed the age of sixty, Washington spoke of his military service: "I'm a super patriot. I went into the army willingly, worked myself up from a lowly private to one of the finest first sergeants you ever saw in your life. An army that treated me like a dog. I couldn't eat in certain places. I couldn't go in certain places. I lived in the worst hovels. I was insulted, berated, used, sacrificed my life, got all kinds of medals, came home a proud soldier. I'm a super patriot."[2]

Harold and Nancy Dorothy Finch never got together again. There were no children.

Like many returning soldiers, Washington took advantage of the GI bill. He enrolled in Chicago's Roosevelt College, a new and innovative institution, one of the few integrated colleges in America at the time. Harold excelled and became a big man on campus. He was elected vice president of the student council and later president. Raymond Clevenger, who was student council president right before Washington, recalled a field trip to the South Side that changed his thinking about race and about Washington, who had accompanied him. Before that visit, Clevenger said, he had never known the conditions of black people. "One of the things about Harold Washington was that he was a very tolerant person. He had lived through that which I was seeing. I never knew him to be a bitter person. He had clearly absorbed all they had done to bright black people, but all the time I knew him he was tolerant of my ignorance. He was willing to let others learn. He was able to understand that a major problem in race relations was ignorance."[3]

Roosevelt College was an exciting place for a young black man right after the war. There were late night bull sessions, usually about civil rights, and demonstrations at local restaurants that refused to serve black students. Two of Harold's classmates were Gus Savage, later to become a newspaper publisher and U.S. congressman, and Dempsey Travis, a future real estate mogul and historian. Travis would write a biography of Harold more than forty years later.

Washington got accepted to Northwestern University Law School where the atmosphere was quite different from his undergraduate days. He was the only African American in his class. He commuted to school each day. In addition to the grind of law school, Harold and some other students supplemented their income with a painting and

---

2 "Remembering Harold," produced by Bill Cameron, *WMAQ Radio.*
3 Raymond Clevenger, "The Road to City Hall," *Chicago Tribune Magazine,* November 16, 1986.

decorating business. He kept a low profile but got his law degree and passed the bar examination. He immediately set up office with his father, Roy Sr., on 47th Street.

They were heady days for a young black lawyer on the South Side of Chicago. Charles Freeman, who would later become an Illinois Supreme Court Justice, was close to Harold then. Freeman came to Chicago from Virginia to attend the John Marshall Law School. He had gotten word that a young black man coming to Chicago would be wise to get affiliated with a local political organization. He had a friend named James Walton who was in the 29th Ward on the West Side. That ward was headed by Bernie Neistein, a tough Jewish guy. Neistein was still the boss even though the ward had gone from predominantly Jewish to predominantly African American. Freeman's guy, Walton, soon made the fatal mistake of running for alderman against the organization. So the new guy in town, Charles Freeman, was forced to leave the 29th Ward.

"I went out to the South Side to the 3rd Ward," Freeman said. "I went out there on a Saturday and there were four guys in the room: Ralph Metcalfe, Harold Washington, John Stroger and Bill Harris. They asked a lot of questions. People wanted to get into that organization because Metcalfe was viewed as a rising star in the black community. Metcalfe was very skeptical of a lawyer coming into his organization. He didn't think lawyers made good precinct workers. But Harold spoke up for me. It was the first time I had met Harold Washington. This was around 1962."[4]

Although it took a while to get to know Harold, Freeman and Washington became lifelong friends. "We officed together for nine or ten years at 63rd and Peoria. We played poker on the weekends, sometimes all night long. Harold was a terrible gambler. He didn't stay in the games long."[5]

Many years later, Charles Freeman would be interviewed by the *Chicago Tribune* and he was very candid about his friend. "Harold did drink. He wasn't a fallen down drunk but he did drink. And he

---

4 Charles Freeman, interviewed by author, Chicago, IL, January 4, 2008.
5 Ibid.

sometimes would disappear for days at a time. No one knew much about Harold's life outside of their own eyesight. I was quoted in the *Tribune* saying complimentary things about him. But I also talked about his habit of not paying bills. Harold was mad. He didn't speak to me for awhile. To me the fact that Harold had changed and had evolved was a story in itself. I think it started in Congress or maybe at the end of his legislative career. He had become a hardworking guy and a dedicated guy. I thought that story was a story young people should hear."[6]

In 1953, Roy Washington died and his 3rd Ward precinct was turned over to Harold by Committeeman Metcalfe. He was good at the political work. He had grown up in it. Like his father before him, he was rewarded with the job of assistant corporation counsel for the city of Chicago.

Harold's career in the corporation counsel's office was unremarkable. In those early years, he had a lot of trouble with jobs. As his friend Charles Freeman put it, "Harold believed the time to show up was for the paycheck." It was a standard joke around the office that Harold was out tending to some matter in Waukegan, up in Lake County. In his defense, though, Harold was not the first Democratic Machine politician to get paid for a no-show job, nor was he the last. Many years later, Washington would tell his biographer, Dempsey J. Travis, a different story about his tenure in the corporation counsel's office. In the spring of 1955, a young Harold Washington was asked to speak at the tenth anniversary of the founding of Roosevelt University. Among the guests were Earl Warren, Chief Justice of the United States, and Eleanor Roosevelt, widow of the late President for whom the university was named. Harold's seat mate on the dais was none other than Richard J. Daley, who had just been elected to his first term as mayor of Chicago. Daley must have been impressed by the young lawyer and the speech he gave that night. According to Harold, the following Monday Corporation Counsel John Melaniphy called him in. He said Mayor Daley liked him and might want to groom him for the position of city prosecutor. Word got around

---

6 Charles Freeman, interviewed by author, Chicago, IL, January 4, 2008.

to other people in the office. There was a subtle period of harassment by whites, according to Harold. It boiled over when Harold got into an argument with a judge who came into his office. There was an angry exchange of words and the hot-tempered Washington threatened to throw the man out the window. That was the beginning of the end. The harassment continued and Washington said he just decided to quit. He said Mayor Daley called him and wished him well.[7]

Yes, Harold Washington had some flaws, but he had a lot of good characteristics too. In the world of Chicago politics, there are two types of people: the money guys, sometimes referred to as the "players", and all the others. Harold was never a money guy. He wasn't interested in the trappings of money, expensive clothes, cars, investments and the like. He never took fancy vacations. He had trouble paying the bills of his modest lifestyle.

Harold Washington liked to hang around saloons and discuss politics and public policy issues. Sometimes he would befuddle companions by mentioning the great book he just read by Benjamin Disraeli, the nineteenth century British author and prime minister.

Still, this intellectual politician was a product of the Democratic Party Machine in Chicago. Throughout his adult life he would be torn between loyalty to the Party organization and his own African American community, which were often at odds during the civil rights movement of the 1960s. When Dr. Martin Luther King, Jr., came to Chicago in 1966 to campaign for open housing, Harold and other black politicians, who owed their jobs and their offices to the Party, were asked to form a committee in support of Mayor Daley. Charles Freeman recalled a time when they attended the first meeting of this group. "We were outside in the car and Harold didn't want to go in. He just didn't want to go. I told him he had to go and he finally did."[8] By the time he got to the state legislature, Washington had become more independent and eventually he would break with the Democratic Machine completely.

---

7 Dempsey J. Travis, *Harold: The People's Mayor* (Chicago: Urban Research Press, Inc., 1989).
8 Charles Freeman, interview.

Harold Washington was elected as state representative in 1964 and he took the oath of office with other members of the seventy-fourth Illinois General Assembly early in the New Year of 1965. Springfield was more of a Southern town than a Northern city in those days. Even though it was the home of Abraham Lincoln, many of its residents sympathized with the Confederacy during the Civil War. Not a whole lot had changed in a hundred years.

The late Corneal Davis told a story about the treatment he received when he first arrived in Springfield as an elected representative in 1946. Davis was a grandson of slaves and had served as a stretcher bearer in World War I. He was a lawyer and a minister of his church. He had been worried about accommodations in Springfield, but a veteran black senator, C.C. Wimbish, told him on the train he could help get him a hotel room. The two legislators walked up to the desk of the Abraham Lincoln Hotel. Davis said everything inside him seemed to drop as the clerk pulled the registration book away and said, "You boys must be new to town or else you wouldn't try to come in here. Before I let any niggers stay in this hotel I'll tear it down!" Davis, who would become a leader and the dean of the Illinois House, and Senator Wimbish had to sleep at the railroad station. They couldn't even get a sandwich downtown and took their meals at a place called Rosalie's on the east side, which was a combination hotel, restaurant, jazz club and whore house.

Things were different when Harold got to Springfield. Black legislators could get hotel rooms. But there was still plenty of racism in town and Harold Washington and his African American colleagues suffered many indignities.

Raymond Ewell, an African American legislator who served with Washington, recalls Harold being in the thick of all the issues important to the black community. He helped establish a black caucus in the house. How much power this group could muster in the beginning was questionable. Many of these legislators held second jobs with the city or county, jobs that were controlled by Mayor Daley and other Party honchos. Ray Ewell remembers when push came to shove on legislation the bosses weren't above calling the wives of black caucus members, telling them hubby was messing with the family income. But, just the fact that blacks were meeting got considerable attention in Springfield. The new black caucus was successful in getting Corneal Davis, a veteran legislator, into the leadership of the house as an assistant majority leader.

During his years in the House, Washington voted with the Party Machine when he had to. He voted against merit selection of judges, and for redistricting plans that insured Party control. He opposed streamlining the state's probation system. Washington was a co-sponsor on bills to legalize prostitution and allowing possession of small amounts of marijuana for private use. He was most proud of his work getting an official state holiday for Dr. Martin Luther King's birthday and his sponsorship of bills strengthening the Fair Employment Practices Commission.

In 1975, there was an historic intraparty struggle for the speakership of the Illinois House. Harold declared himself a candidate for the post even though he only had two votes: his own and another member of the black caucus, Lewis Caldwell. Mayor Daley was supporting Clyde Choate from downstate Anna, Illinois. Choate was viewed as an old line party power broker from the camp of Paul Powell, a legendary Secretary of State whose office issued driver licenses and license plates. Following his death, eight hundred thousand dollars in cash was found in shoe boxes in Powell's residential hotel suite. Independents were backing William Redmond, who had the distinction of being the Democratic Party Chairman of the heavily Republican DuPage County, west of the city. Governor Walker, a maverick Democrat and opponent of the Daley Machine, had his own candidate. The roll calls dragged on through most of the month of January but Choate couldn't muster the required votes. Finally, Daley threw his support to Redmond, as did Harold Washington. Eventually, on the ninety-third roll call, seven Republicans crossed over and gave the Independent, Redmond, a victory. Harold was given a chairmanship of the House Judiciary Committee. One black Chicago legislator, Raymond Ewell, stuck with Clyde Choate through all the roll calls. When asked why, Ewell replied, "I gave him my word and that means something to me."

In 1976, Harold Washington got a chance to run for the Illinois Senate. A vacancy occurred when Senate President Cecil Partee decided to make an ill-fated run for Attorney General. By this time, Mayor Daley was leery of Washington's streaks of independence but Partee convinced him to go with Harold. No sooner was he sworn in as a senator than he jumped into another battle of leadership. Thomas Hynes, a loyal Daley Democrat from the 19th Ward on the South Side, had the backing of Party leaders for the Senate presidency. But dissidents in that chamber held back enough votes to keep Hynes from the prize. Among the dissidents were freshman Senator Harold Washington and the black caucus. They wanted the right to choose their own black representative for the leadership team instead of the Party hack that Hynes had selected. This time there were more than one hundred roll calls. Finally Hynes caved in and compromised with the dissidents. The black caucus got what it wanted. Harold Washington was becoming a force to be reckoned with in Chicago politics.

In the race for Senate president, Harold Washington was the candidate of the black caucus. Within a couple of months he would be a candidate for mayor of Chicago in the special election to fill the unexpired term of Richard J. Daley. Harold came in third behind Alderman Roman Pucinski and the winner, Michael Bilandic. Even though he received only 11% of the vote, Washington and other African American leaders were designing number configurations that might give a black candidate the edge in a three-way contest for mayor in the future.

One of the insults to the black community in Chicago, and there were many of them, was detailed in a *Chicago Tribune* series published in the early '70s. In one of the finer works of journalism in that period, a team of *Tribune* reporters worked for five months uncovering hundreds of incidents of police beatings and misconduct against citizens, mostly African Americans. The reporters interviewed hundreds of victims and witnesses, even conducting thorough lie detector tests. While some were found to be lying to cover their own misdeeds, the overwhelming majority of victims tested as telling the truth. And the *Tribune* backed up their stories by tracking down witnesses. The newspaper chronicled some brutal beatings given by police to persons involved in minor traffic violations. The stories may not have had the impact of incidents captured on videotape in later years, but they were vivid enough. One of the victims was Dr. Herbert Odom, a dentist who was roughed up during a minor traffic stop. Odom happened to be a friend of Congressman Ralph Metcalfe, the committeeman of the 3rd Ward.

Ralph Metcalfe's son had been a student activist at Columbia University in the '60s. He had urged his father to break with the Machine because of its insensitivity to the needs of blacks. This and the Odom incident finally caused the longtime Machine loyalist and sponsor of Harold Washington to break with his Party. "It's never too late to be black," he told one audience.

Before long, Mayor Daley took Metcalfe's patronage away and put up candidates against him for both ward committeeman and Congress. Metcalfe survived these challenges but Harold had remained neutral, which probably explains Metcalfe's refusal to support Harold in his 1977 bid for mayor. In 1978, the Party did not oppose Metcalfe in the March primary election and he seemed headed for an easy victory in the November election. But on October 10, the veteran congressman was found dead of a heart attack in his South Side apartment. The Democratic Party named Bennett Stewart, a former alderman and Party loyalist, to replace Metcalfe on the ticket. Stewart won and went off to Washington.

Harold's unsuccessful run for mayor in 1977 was his final split with the Democratic Machine. He said he should have done it years before and vowed to wage war with the organization. So no one was surprised in 1980 when Harold decided to challenge the incumbent congressman in the first district, Bennett Stewart. Harold defeated Stewart and two other primary opponents.

Washington's election to the Congress of the United States was a milestone in a long political career. He was fifty-eight years old. The salary and benefits were the best of his life, not to mention the prestige. He was stimulated intellectually. Politics was never a certainty, especially when you were bucking the Machine, but it looked like Harold had a safe seat for as long as he wanted it.

He arrived in Washington with a new president, Ronald Reagan, and soon became one of the new administration's chief antagonists. He loved railing against Reaganomics and what it was doing to the black community.

When Chicago's black leaders turned to Harold Washington as the best bet to carry the torch for mayor in 1983, he was reluctant. A major split was happening in the Democratic Party between the followers of Mayor Jane Byrne and State's Attorney Richard M. Daley. This was the kind of split that might give an African American a real chance to win the Mayor's Office. But Harold still balked. He demanded large sums of money for the campaign and large numbers of newly registered voters. An inspired black community provided both.

Two crucial events would haunt Harold Washington's political life and surface time and again to jeopardize his attempts for higher office. One was the suspension of his law license in 1970 for accepting fees from clients and failing to perform the legal work. The other was his jailing for thirty-six days in 1972 for failing to file federal income tax returns. Both of these transgressions involved small sums of money and probably could have been resolved easily. It remains a mystery why a person as politically astute as Harold Washington let them slide and become a permanent part of his record.

A cleaning woman named Ella Liggins complained that she paid Washington $50 to handle her divorce case but he did nothing. There were other similar divorce cases and someone who complained that Harold failed to show up in traffic court after they paid a fee. For two years, a grievance committee of the Chicago Bar Association tried to get a written response from Washington or have him appear at hearings. Washington ignored everything. Eventually he told the committee the clients hadn't paid all of the fees that were due and that he wasn't certain he didn't perform some of the services. He did acknowledge negligence in not responding to the committee sooner. The Illinois Supreme Court suspended his law license for one year. It would be six years before Harold got it back.

The tax matter was also a strange affair. The federal government accused Washington of failure to file returns for four years during the 1960s. Washington claimed he owed nothing. The government said he owed about eight thousand dollars. The matter was eventually settled for fifteen hundred dollars. Harold had to plead no contest and serve a short jail sentence. The federal judge in the case said that if Harold had come in and filed the back returns immediately, there would have been no need for a jail sentence. Some of Washington's supporters still say he was a victim of the Nixon administration, that he was being punished for leading a walkout of black legislators when Vice President Spiro Agnew spoke to the Illinois General Assembly in May of 1971. Many years later, the *Chicago Tribune* would debunk that theory, noting the Washington investigation began during the Johnson administration and his indictment occurred six weeks before the Agnew appearance.

Whatever his past problems, Harold Washington was now the overwhelming choice of Chicago's revived African American community to be their candidate for mayor.

✴ CHAPTER 5 ✴

Richard M. Daley

THE YEAR IS 1971 *and I'm sent to cover a debate in the contest for mayor of the city of Chicago. The debate is sponsored by the Junior League Club, a group of young women socialites on the near North Side of Chicago. One of the debaters is Richard Fried-man, a former Democrat whom the Republican Party has chosen to oppose the reelection of Richard J. Daley. Friedman is a good government type. He is head of the Better Government Association, which regularly probes corruption and malfeasance in local govern-ment. But Friedman won't be debating the great Richard J. Daley today. He's too much of an underdog. The boss has sent a surro-gate to engage Mr. Friedman: his son, Richard M. Daley. The son is a twenty-eight-year-old attorney who has been a delegate to the state constitutional convention but has not yet held elective office. I'm thinking my assignment is not a very good one because I know too well that old Richard J. is the real newsmaker in town. And it turns out I'm right. Young Daley bombs in the debate. He struggles with even the basic questions. I figure the Christian Brothers at De La Salle High School (where Daley and his father went to school) put more emphasis on management skills rather than elocution. By contrast, Friedman is smooth and has command of the issues. He's a handsome man, an outdoors man, whose hobby is hot air balloon-ing. Henry Hanson of the* Chicago Daily News *led a story about Friedman's candidacy with this question: "Is Chicago ready for a divorced, Jewish balloonist?" Daley is painful to watch. I'm almost embarrassed to roll the camera. The debate wasn't much of a news story. And after all, Richard J. Daley rolled to a huge victory that year. But I remember young Daley hanging in there despite being so uncomfortable. The kid showed courage. Richard Friedman went on to a successful law practice.*

Rich Daley was an unlikely politician. He had little, if any, ability for public speaking. He was shy. He wasn't good at glad handing and had no talent for putting on the phony smile. He would not do the easy things politicians do to be successful. He would not pick up the phone to make small talk with someone who might help him. He would not speak with people he didn't like or go to events if he knew people he didn't like would be there. He just wasn't much of a mixer.

Yet Richard M. Daley had a first rate political mind. His apprenticeship was done with one of America's masters. And, of course, he had inherited the political brand name. Daley and his younger brothers would grow up in a very privileged political atmosphere. They would accompany their father to the Democratic National Convention in Los Angeles in 1960 that nominated John F. Kennedy for president. Rich and his friends from Providence College, while visiting New York, would use U.N. Ambassador Adlai Stevenson's suite at the Waldorf Towers. Later, the family would overnight at the Lyndon Johnson White House and young Richard would walk the Rose Garden with the president.[1]

Right after law school, young Daley's political training would continue as a delegate to the state constitutional convention, and then it was on to his father's seat in the Illinois Senate, a position held when the elder Daley died suddenly in 1976. Daley was then elected committeeman of the 11th Ward to fill his father's vacancy.

Daley's early career in the Senate was highlighted by petty political maneuvers aimed at annoying the Senate's independent Democrats, all of whom were constant critics of his father. In 1977, *Chicago* Magazine named Richard M. Daley one of the ten worst legislators in the General Assembly. A panel of reporters, legislators, lobbyists, and state employees gave him the honor for what

---

1 Ciccone, *Daley: Power and Presidential Politics.*

they described as arrogance, shark-like qualities and living off his father's name. They said that if his name was Richie M. Schwartz he wouldn't even be in the legislature.[2]

But Daley's life would change dramatically. After the death of his father and the struggle for succession, and after Mayor Jane Byrne waged war against him, a new Daley emerged. The son of the last of the big city bosses became, of all things, a "Goo Goo" (good government type) as the South Side Machine people like to call the lakefront liberals.

When his son Kevin was born with spina bifida, it had a profound effect on Daley and his family. He was torn between duties in Springfield and wanting to be with his gravely ill son.

By now he was a serious senator. He led the fight for legislation to end nursing home abuses. He voted against pay raises for legislators. He went up against Mayor Byrne and Governor Thompson in a battle to end the state sales tax on food and medicine. He was appointed Chairman of the Judiciary Committee.

And Senator Daley began mending fences with the independent Democrats. He appeared at a softball game sponsored by Senator Dawn Clark Netsch. Netsch was a prominent liberal and former law professor who had once referred to Daley as "dirty little Richie." They made up.

In 1979, Daley announced he would run for Cook County State's Attorney. He surprised many friends, some of whom thought he would run for County Clerk. The *Tribune* had reported earlier that Daley was considering Clerk of the Circuit Court, a position laden with patronage jobs. It would put him in a position to help 11th Ward comrades who had been displaced by Mayor Byrne. But in the end it was State's Attorney.

Richard M. Daley, son of the last of the big city Democratic bosses, was now an independent Democrat. He would not seek the endorsement of the Democratic Party. Byrne would put up Alderman Edward Burke to oppose him in the primary. Burke would also receive the endorsement of former Mayor Michael Bilandic.

---

2 William Brashler and Joyce Hansen, *Chicago Magazine,* February 1983.

Daley began building a countywide organization. He mailed out postcards asking for help in his fight to end the sales tax on food and medicine. The response was huge. Devotees of his late father and their sons and daughter offered support. A new countywide organization was emerging.

An interesting melodrama, embarrassing to Daley, would unfold during this campaign. It involved the death of Fire Commissioner Robert J. Quinn early in 1979. Quinn had been forced to resign under Mayor Bilandic amidst charges of mismanagement for using money from the widows and orphans fund to finance the department's marching band.

Robert J. Quinn was a colorful and controversial Chicago character during his twenty-one years as head of the fire department. He was a boyhood friend of Mayor Richard J. Daley, who elevated him to the top job in 1956. As a firefighter he was a bona fide hero, rescuing people from burning buildings. He once threw a two-hundred-pound woman over his shoulder while her clothes were burning and then jumped four feet to an adjacent building. In the Navy in World War II he had been decorated for his efforts battling a three day aviation fuel fire aboard the tanker *Montana*. He was a physical fitness enthusiast who neither drank nor smoked. A lifelong bachelor, he did have a weakness for young women, sometimes showing up at a wake with a beauty queen half his age. This did not go over well with the wives of the firemen. There was an occasion when a nineteen-year-old woman suffered smoke inhalation during a fire in an apartment rented to Commissioner Quinn. There were some sketchy explanations that the woman was a niece from Ireland or a friend of a friend.

Then there was the time in 1959 when Quinn ordered the sounding of the city's emergency warning sirens when the White Sox clinched the pennant. And he was roundly criticized for showing off his physically fit firefighters jogging down the Kennedy Expressway and causing massive traffic jams. Critics labeled him a bigot for having few African Americans on the department. When asked about it, Quinn said it seemed that mostly Polish and Irish applied for the job; blacks didn't like heat or smoke. He was given some high marks as an innovator for pioneering the use of snorkels, boats and helicopters in firefighting.

In the fall of 1979, reporter Dick Kay with producer Joseph P. Howard of WMAQ-TV presented a series of reports alleging some shenanigans in connection with the disposition of Quinn's estate. A nurse from Mercy Hospital, who tended to Quinn before his death, told of Michael Daley and a doctor coming to Quinn's bedside and guiding his hand while he signed some legal documents. Indeed, after his death, it was revealed the Commissioner had signed over a house valued at eighty thousand dollars to Patricia Daley, daughter of the late mayor. Two bank accounts valued at fifty thousand dollars were signed over to Senator Richard M. Daley. There was also a farm near Lake Geneva, Wisconsin, valued at two hundred thousand dollars which Quinn had signed over to a longtime assistant. Michael Daley, executor of the Quinn estate, threatened to sue Channel 5 for libel.

A niece appeared. Quinn's only living relative and legal heir came forward and contested the will. The case dragged on through the campaign for State's Attorney. A federal investigation was conducted but United States Attorney Thomas Sullivan eventually found no violations of federal law. In the end the case was settled. The niece was given over ninety thousand dollars and the rest of the estate was divided among the Daleys and a few others. No libel suit was ever filed against the television station that broke the story. Dick Kay and Joe Howard received an Emmy award for their reporting.

The primary campaign for State's Attorney was a lively one, as evidenced by this news commentary I wrote at the time:

"Shots are fired at Eddie Burke's campaign headquarters. At a Democratic precinct captain's rally, the voice of the late Mayor Daley is heard from the balcony. The captains are momentarily shocked but it's only a prank, someone with a tape recorder and amplifier. Also a prank, the Rich Daley balloons that float through the air. It brings back memories of past elections when Eddie Hanrahan, who had been dumped by the party as State's Attorney, placed fortune cookies on the precinct captains' table, 'Vote for Hanrahan' inside each cookie. Then there was the time John Hoellen, a GOP candidate

for mayor, brought a live snake to City Hall, implying he was the man to drive the snakes out. A distraught Bridgeport woman calls a newsroom to say Mayor Byrne is sending the building inspectors down on a church where Rich Daley is supposed to speak. In the final week of the campaign, signs are being torn down and put back up again. Preposterous lies are being told about the candidates on little mimeographed sheets. Threats are being made. A keen observer notes that campaigning in Chicago hasn't changed much since the turn of the century when 'Hinky Dink' Kenna and 'Bathhouse' John Coughlin ruled the 1st Ward and, according to the old song, 'there were biters and fighters and Irish dynamiters on the streets of Chicago'."

Rich Daley perfected the Columbo look, after the popular TV detective. The rumpled raincoat, the stumbling speech. But sincerity came through. The voters liked him and he won easily. Daley's victory over Burke, by better than two to one, was sweet. He not only beat Burke handily, he sent a strong message to Mayor Byrne that the Daley name was still solid in Chicago and Cook County.

Winning the general election would be a much more difficult task. The incumbent State's Attorney was Republican Bernard Carey. Clean cut and looking like an altar boy, Carey was a former FBI agent who had been elected with heavy African American support following Edward Hanrahan's ill-fated raid of a Black Panther Party headquarters in 1969. Two Panther leaders, Fred Hampton and Mark Clark, were killed.

Carey also had the support of liberal Democrats. One of his chief advisors was Don Rose, the guru of independent politics in Chicago.

The contest was tight all the way. A *Sun Times* straw poll in October showed Daley with a lead of just over one percentage point. In his campaign commercials, Carey brought up the controversy over the Quinn estate. They showed an elderly woman, interviewed on the street, saying she still has too many questions about what happened to Commissioner Quinn's money. Daley hired Washington media consultant Robert Squier and focused his campaign commercials on fighting drugs. Toward the end of the campaign, Richard

M. Daley would find support from some unlikely sources. One of them was *Chicago Sun Times* columnist Mike Royko.

Mike Royko was the premier newspaper columnist in Chicago. Some political experts believed his opinions could influence an election by as much as twenty points. He was the chief critic of the Democratic Machine and its leader, Richard J. Daley, sometimes likening the Daley sons to the Three Stooges. But in the campaign for State's Attorney, Royko sided with young Daley. And he wrote several columns favorable to Daley and critical of Carey. In one column he described Carey as "the mouse who wants to be a lion."

Why Royko favored Daley in this instance is open to speculation. It might have been the columnist's natural instinct to favor the under-dog. Some of Royko's friends believe he was mad at Carey because of a 1977 barroom disturbance for which Royko was prosecuted and fined a thousand dollars for disorderly conduct and misdemeanor assault. Then there was Phil Krone, a crafty political operative and Daley advisor who often had Royko's ear. Others thought Robert Bill-ings, a tough former *Daily News* reporter, had an influence on Royko. He had signed on to the Daley campaign. Whatever or whomever it was, Royko came out swinging on behalf of Richard M. Daley.

A source who worked on the Daley campaign offered another explanation. One of Daley's people was making anonymous phone calls to Royko. Royko often picked up his own telephone and dis-coursed with the general public. Sometimes the conversations were brief and caustic. Other times the columnist would listen and argue a bit. A Daley field operative began making anonymous phone calls to Royko after Royko had written something favorable about Daley. The conversation would go something like this:

Daley worker: "How much did Daley pay you to write that article?"

Royko: "Who the fuck is this?"

Daley worker: "Fuck you, Royko. You're in Daley's pocket. You're just an ass kisser."

Royko: "I don't know who you are, you son of a bitch. Come on down here and say that to my face."

Daley worker: "Fuck you, old man, you're just an ass kisser."

Then, according to the source, another column favorable to Daley would appear in the paper.

Despite the help from Royko, the contest stayed close all the way to the end. After the primary, Mayor Byrne endorsed Daley. But it didn't stick. Throughout the general election campaign she kept sniping at him and praising his opponent. Finally she withdrew her endorsement, accusing him of a complicated scheme to prevent minorities from buying homes in the 11th Ward. Bernie Carey found himself in the awkward position of defending his opponent, saying the Byrne charges were unfair.

Eleanor "Sis" Daley, widow of the late mayor, was a matriarchal figure in Chicago. Dignified and poised, she had always kept a low profile. Some believed she was part of the brain power that contributed to her husband's success. She had tremendous influence over the mayor and her children. She convinced Mayor Daley to spare the old landmark Chicago Public Library from the wrecking ball and turn it into a cultural center. One time Mayor Daley was seen on television berating an opposing alderman and telling him to get a haircut. When he got home that night, Sis told him he was out of line and he ought to apologize. Daley made the call.

Phil Krone, the wily political handler in the Daley for State's Attorney race, came up with an idea. Krone had seen surveys showing Mrs. Daley to be held in higher esteem than the Cardinal Archbishop of Chicago. Why not tap that reservoir of good will on television? He went to Bill Daley, who liked the idea but said that he, Krone, would have to approach his mother. "I told Mrs. Daley I didn't mind losing an election if we had done everything we could to win, but I did mind losing if we had resources and didn't use them,"[3] Krone said. Sis Daley graciously accepted the assignment.

It's a cold Friday night in November and I'm at home in front of the fire with a nice cocktail and a good book. The phone rings. It's the office. A young and very excited producer tells me we've got an exclusive interview with Mrs. Richard J. Daley tomorrow. He says they've specifically requested me to do the interview. I'm a little bit

---

3   Phil Krone, interviewed by author, Chicago, IL, November 19, 2007.

suspicious and remind the producer there's an election on Tuesday and Mrs. Daley's boy is locked in a very tight race. Still, it is Mrs. Richard J. Daley. Over the years she has rarely granted interviews. The meeting is scheduled for the next morning at the Daley home on South Lowe Avenue in the heart of the bungalow and two flat belt. I sit down in the living room with Mrs. Daley. My cameraman is Jim Stricklin, who is fascinated by the portrait painting of Mayor Daley over the fireplace. He keeps zooming in and out as Mrs. Daley and I make some small talk about her late husband and their life together in politics, how he made it a point to take time for her and the seven children during his busy career. Occasionally he came home for lunch and rarely missed dinner. She says she is very proud of Richard. He's never lowered himself and has run a good campaign. He's a good, honest man. He would make a fine State's Attorney. His father would be proud of him. I give her a chance to go after Mayor Byrne. She only says she doesn't understand the attacks the mayor has made on her son and that they're very hurtful to her as a mother. When asked if her son is interested in running for mayor, she says she has never heard him say he wanted to run for mayor, and, after all, there are better positions than mayor. Mrs. Daley is smooth and charming and cautious.

The exclusive interview with Mrs. Richard J. Daley wasn't that exclusive. It turns out that other exclusive interviews were granted to selected reporters from Channels 2, 7 and 9. Phil Krone, mastermind of the "Mrs. Daley strategy", scored big. The weekend before the election for State's Attorney, you couldn't turn on a television newscast without seeing the much admired Mrs. Eleanor "Sis" Daley. On Tuesday, Richard M. Daley was elected Cook County State's Attorney over Bernard Carey by just sixteen thousand votes. Over two million votes were cast.

Rich Daley, his wife Maggie and their three children lived in a bungalow on South Emerald Avenue in the Bridgeport neighborhood within a few blocks of where Daley had grown up and where his mother still lived.

The youngest son, Kevin, had been afflicted with spina bifida since birth and the family converted the dining room into a nursery for the boy. It was close to the parents' first floor bedroom. Although the disease had left the infant unable to hear or speak, he could make enough sound to let his mom and dad know if he was in pain. There were many trips to the hospital.

One night in the late winter of 1981, the child was rushed to Children's Memorial Hospital. His parents were at his bedside when Kevin died, at the age of two and a half. Two children remained, Nora and Patrick, and later Mrs. Daley would give birth to another daughter, Lalley. The tragedy would weigh heavily on the young family. The nursery in the dining room would stay the same for a long time. The crib and the clothing and the toys would not be touched.

Bernard E₁

IN CHICAGO ON ELECTION DAY, it's a very bad omen when a ward boss gets a call from a precinct captain who proclaims, "They're dancin'." This means the captain has dutifully observed the feet of the voters at his polling place when they are behind the curtain in the act of voting. If the feet are moving too much and the voter is taking too much time, it means he or she is picking and choosing candidates instead of pulling the straight party lever.

At the age of nineteen, Bernard Epton was a Republican precinct captain in the 7th Ward on the South Side of Chicago. As he liked to tell the story years later, one of the party bosses caught *him* dancing in the polling place and he was fired summarily.

Bernie's father, Arthur I. Epton, left Germany when he was thirteen years old. He went first to England where he worked for a time and learned how to speak the English language, and then it was on to America where A.I. Epton, as he came to be known in the world of business, made quite a career for himself. He started first in the jewelry business and later found his way into reclaimed rubber, buying excess rubber from the large manufacturers in Akron, Ohio, and reselling it for rubber sheets and matting.

He was a flamboyant character who loved fashionable clothes and the fast lanes of American business in the early twentieth century. He was a persistent dealmaker, but more than once things went sour and he would find himself tapped out financially. Then there would be traveling and more deals and a comeback. Epton's religion was you don't have to have a religion as long as you meet

. He always paid back everything he owed. There was
oo. Epton and his wife Rose were married in 1907. They
the South Shore neighborhood and had four children:
laine, Bernie and Jerry.

uth Shore Chicago in the '20s and '30s was an interesting mix
upwardly mobile Irish and Jews who outnumbered other ethnic
groups. They got along well together and the Epton boys had many
Irish friends. The Irish and the Jews of South Shore also had a
common bond. Most of them were Democrats, loyal to the Democratic Machine of Chicago and Cook County. But the Eptons were
an exception. A.I. Epton was a devout Republican who didn't like
President Franklin D. Roosevelt.

According to the youngest son Jerry, Saul was the sweet one in
the family. "Bernie was the renegade. He was always arguing with
my father. They loved each other but they were always arguing.
My sister Elaine was that other Epton brother with the long hair.
My dad said I was the dumbest of the four so he took me into the
business. We were in rubber but later we got into plastics. He fired
me one day 'cause I said to him: Gee, Dad, this is easy. All you do
is buy a piece of material and then resell it for double the price.
And he said: Is that right? Get your ass out of here. Now you're my
competitor. I had a wife and a child and he threw me out of the
business. I was out of work for six months and eventually I would
come back to him. I was a smart alec punk kid. He was teaching
me a lesson. And he eventually let me run it, A.I. Epton and Sons.
I was the only son. My brothers were never in it."[1]

Bernie was the bright boy of the Epton family. He graduated from
Hyde Park High School at the age of fifteen. He had gone briefly
to Morgan Park Military Academy but the military regimen did not
suit his independent nature. He had a great love for baseball. He
was never good enough to play on a high school team but he was
very active in neighborhood softball leagues.

"Bernie had a team sponsored by the *Chicago Herald-American*,"
recalls brother Jerry. "Bernie was the captain. He owned the bat

---

1   Jerry Epton, interviewed by author, October 13, 2008, October 31, 2008.

and ball and, if he didn't want you on the team, forget it. That was Bernie. He loved baseball and the White Sox. There was a kid named Bob Meyers who Bernie wouldn't let on the team. He was a boxer and he and Bernie had a showdown at the field house at O'Keefe Elementary School. They put the gloves on. Meyers beat a tattoo on my brother. I was crying and the guys were all standing around and Bernie raised his head and told Meyers he still wasn't on the goddamned team. That was Bernie. If he had a principle, there was no deviation from it. And that doesn't make a good politician."[2]

The Epton family lived in a nice six-flat on South Merrill Avenue. Down the street, on Seventy-First Street, was Rosenblum's Drug Store, where everyone hung out, including Bernie, who had a part time job there. The owner of the store, Les Rosenblum, had no family of his own. He loved Bernie and wanted him to go to pharmacy school and come into the business. Bernie said no. He was going into law. He also said no to his father, who offered him money to join A.I. Epton and Sons. Bernie knew early on that law was what he wanted.

"My brother was very strong-willed," said Jerry Epton. "I think when he was a young man he thought he could be President of the United States. He suffered from violent headaches that sometimes would send him to bed. When he was just a boy he was riding on a truck with a guy named Mickey Freeman and fell off, hitting his head. After that, my mother, in her old fashioned way, would say that Bernie was 'cracked' whenever he had headaches."[3]

The Depression years were tough for A.I. Epton's business. Young Bernie, who had started college at Northwestern, was forced to go to work at the Western Pipe and Steel Company in suburban Blue Island, Illinois. Sister Elaine had to forgo a college education and go to work.

Epton would eventually graduate from the University of Chicago and DePaul University Law School. But law school was interrupted. The family all cried when Bernie enlisted in the U.S. Army Air Corps.

---

2   Jerry Epton, interview.
3   Ibid.

He ended up in England with the Eighth Air Force as a navigator on the B-17 Flying Fortress. During World War II the Eighth Air Force would suffer severe casualties, fifty-four thousand killed or taken prisoner. Epton was one of the lucky survivors due in part, no doubt, to the skills of his ship's captain, Colonel Charles E. "Bud" Rohr of California. Bernie thought Colonel Rohr was sensational because he always managed to get the ship across the channel and back to base after it had been crippled by anti-aircraft fire. In England, Epton met a beautiful woman, Audrey, who would later become his wife. Bernie kept in touch with Colonel Rohr after the war and, through him, met some new California friends, including an up-and-coming young Syrian-American comedian from Toledo named Danny Thomas.

Bernie Epton was part of that wave of optimism that returning veterans brought to America right after World War II. They were imbued with a sense that most anything could be accomplished in the good old US of A through hard work and dedication. Epton came home with a chest full of ribbons. He had attained the rank of captain. He got back into politics, still as a Republican. The prominent Democratic Party leader, Colonel Jacob Arvey, once approached Saul and Bernie Epton. "This is Chicago," he told them. "It's a Democratic town. Come on over here and everything will be fine." But Bernie was adamant. He was going to do it his way. And the Epton brothers remained in the GOP. Brother Jerry Epton put it this way: "With Bernie, if you said green, he'd say blue. Then he'd proceed to show you how blue was correct."[4]

He helped found a successful law firm that advised and defended insurance companies. The Epton family settled in Hyde Park, the only integrated neighborhood in Chicago after the war. Soon there would be a family, two boys and two girls. The children attended public schools. For many years after the war, Epton would not set foot in an airplane. Jerry Epton remembers hiring his brother to represent him in a patent dispute with a company back East. They traveled to Philadelphia by train to appear in court.

---

4   Jerry Epton, interview.

Bernie became involved in his community. He was the lawyer for the South Shore Chamber of Commerce. The stunning Audrey was a busy mom and housewife, but found time to appear in B'Nai B'rtih fashion shows. After the West Side rioting in 1966, Epton brought suit against the city and the county on behalf of local merchants to recover property losses they sustained in the turmoil. He was elected to the legislature as a Republican in 1966. At that time, Illinois had a one-hundred-ten-year-old system of electing state House members that was unique for the entire nation. Each district could elect three representatives. There was a complex practice of cumulative voting. But the bottom line was a Republican could get elected in heavily Democratic districts in Chicago while Democrats could be elected in Republican areas in the suburbs and downstate. There were three representatives in each district, two always going to the dominant party. The idea was to have one minority party member elected in each district. It turned out that some of the best legislators were these minority party members. Bernie Epton was one of them.

He stood over six feet tall. A neat beard offset his bald head. Some of his admirers even described him as Lincolnesque in appearance. He was well tailored and might have been mistaken for a professor at the University of Chicago. He was known for his extra dry wit. In the legislature, he gained a reputation as a progressive who supported civil rights issues. He gave generously to African American charities. On the issue of civil rights, the Republican from Hyde Park was probably more liberal than many of his Democratic colleagues.

In Springfield, Bernie was a loner. He had his own apartment. Never much of a drinker, Epton rarely appeared on the nightlife scene, which was quite lively when the legislature was in session and hundreds of mostly male lawmakers and lobbyists were in town.

During the lengthy sessions, Epton would sometimes take refuge in the Republican leadership office where he might engage in conversations with young staffers or lie on the couch and suffer through one of his frequent migraines.

Bernie had a flare for dramatic big ideas. Once he tried to put together a deal to purchase the Chicago White Sox. One of his partners was Danny Thomas. Thomas, who got his big break starring at a place called the 5100 Club on North Broadway in Chicago, was now a Hollywood star. A couple of other stars, Bing Crosby and Bob Hope, also had ownership positions in major league franchises. Epton's group made an offer to buy a majority of the team's stock for $4.8 million. The offer was rejected. Bernie wanted to sue the White Sox but Danny Thomas wanted no part of that.

Epton became the Illinois House expert on insurance law. He was named chairman of the Insurance Committee. At the time, Illinois ranked second in the nation for bankruptcies of insurance companies. The companies that failed were usually small and they offered low premiums. Their customers were poor. Over a fifteen-year period, the policyholders lost $80 million. Epton sponsored legislation requiring the insurance industry to create a fund that would pay the claims of policyholders whose company had gone under. Many of the consumer protection laws on insurance in Illinois were the result of Epton's legislative work.

As a GOP legislator from the liberal Hyde Park area, Epton fit in well. Robert Mann, a Democrat and champion of liberal causes, called Epton a "diverse and very bright person. He became very compassionate on social issues."[5]

Epton could also be a hard nosed politician. Early in 1973, Republicans, who had retained a majority in the Illinois House, were about the task of reelecting their speaker and other leaders. But there was a problem. The incumbent speaker, W. Robert Blair, had antagonized many in his own party in the previous session. A dissident group formed under the leadership of Representative Henry Hyde from Park Ridge, a sleepy, close-in suburb of Chicago later to become famous as the hometown of First Lady Hillary Rodham Clinton. Hyde had enough votes to hold up Blair's election but not enough to win himself. Finally a deal was worked out. Hyde and the dissidents were given a couple of leadership posts

5   *Chicago Tribune,* December 14, 1987.

and some other concessions for their votes. But shortly after his election, Blair reneged. The Hyde people cried foul and double cross to no avail. Bernie Epton was with Speaker Blair and was one of the masterminds of the scheme. Henry Hyde quit the legislature the next year and got elected to the U.S. Congress, where he became a conservative icon. Many years later he would gain fame as chairman of the Judiciary Committee, which brought articles of impeachment against President William Jefferson Clinton.

In the 1960s, Bernard Epton, the successful lawyer, legislator and community booster, faced a problem that was worrying parents all over America. Their children were in total rebellion and out of control. The American dream, which the parents had worked so hard to achieve, was totally repugnant to the kids. They were turning on to drugs and dropping out of conventional society. Their goals were lofty and idealistic but certainly hard to argue about. The main thing they wanted was world peace, an end to the current war in Vietnam and civil rights for black Americans. What aggravated the parents were the tactics: civil disobedience, demonstrations that violated the property rights of others, burning of draft cards. Moms and dads didn't like the long hair and the music either.

One of these so-called flower children was Bernie Epton's oldest son, Jeff, who had been born in 1948. Jeff was frequently involved in protest demonstrations against the war in Vietnam. The father and the son would have many bitter disputes during the 1960s. Bernie even sought professional counseling to help resolve the family discord. Jeff says he believes he was drafted because of his anti-war activities. So he went to Canada and he stayed there about six months. Before he left, Bernie gave him five thousand dollars. He said, "I don't agree with what you're doing but your grandfather would have wanted you to have this money, even though your grandfather would not have agreed with what you're doing." Jeff thinks this was a lot of bull. He believes his dad wanted to give him the five thousand because he was worried about him. The money didn't last long in Canada.

When Dr. Martin Luther King, Jr., was murdered in 1968, Epton took his other son, Mark, to Memphis and marched with black sanitation workers on the day of King's funeral. In 1983, Bernard Epton made a decision to run for the office of mayor of Chicago. It wasn't such a bad idea to begin with. A Republican hadn't been elected mayor since the 1920s. The Democratic organization had been in disarray since the death of Mayor Daley in 1976. The current mayor, Jane Byrne, was a maverick who had defeated the Democratic Machine but now had her own political liabilities. Governor James Thompson called and urged him to do it. So Bernie took the plunge in the hope that he might be a viable alternative to the warring Democrats. Bernie Epton, the urbane lawyer-legislator, the supporter of civil rights legislation and minority causes, would soon be called a racist.

Harold Washington campaigning at Cabrini Green Public Housing. *(Courtesy WMAQ-TV NBC 5 News Chicago)*

Harold's victory speech: "I can't tell you how happy I am…history was made tonight." *(Courtesy WMAQ-TV NBC 5 News Chicago)*

Mayor Jane Byrne campaigning for reelection. *(Courtesy WMAQ-TV NBC 5 News Chicago)*

Richard M. Daley in the primary election campaign. *(Courtesy WMAQ-TV NBC 5 News Chicago)*

Bernard Epton, the GOP candidate for Mayor. *(Courtesy WMAQ-TV NBC 5 News Chicago)*

Edward Vrdolyak, the Democratic chairman who supported Mayor Byrne. *(Courtesy WMAQ-TV NBC 5 News Chicago)*

Mayor Richard J. Daley with the author in 1975.

The three Democratic candidates took part in four debates before the primary. *(Courtesy WTTW Chicago)*

PART III

Campaign!

★ CHAPTER 7 ★

Street Soldiers

JAMES "SKINNY" SHEAHAN is one of the great characters of Chicago politics. He could have been in New York or Boston or Philadelphia. Everyone who lives in one of those cities and is involved in politics knows someone like him. But Skinny Sheahan belongs to Chicago. Born and raised in the 19th Ward on the South Side, he came from a family of eight children.

His brother Mike was the star of the family. Handsome and athletic, Mike Sheahan became a Chicago policeman, later was elected alderman and then served as Sheriff of Cook County for sixteen years. Big Ten football fans might remember him as a Saturday game official who occasionally worked the Rose Bowl.

Skinny insists that his father favored brother Mike and delights in imitating Dad at the dinner table in Irish brogue: "Now you boys'll be saving some extra potatoes for Mike, he's got a game tomorrow." Thus Skinny became skinny.

Like many young Irish-American men of his era, James Sheahan went to the seminary for high school and one year of college but then decided against the priesthood, finished college at St. Joe's of Indiana and ended up teaching eighth grade for the Chicago Board of Education on the South Side.

Skinny says he caught the political bug in 1971 when a sister-in-law asked him to help William Singer, an independent Democrat, who was running against the Machine in the 43rd Ward on the North Side. Singer won.

Later he joined brother Mike in another aldermanic race in their home 19th Ward. The Sheahan brothers got behind Jeremiah Joyce, who was opposing the chosen candidate of the regular Democratic Party. Joyce won.

Skinny worked on many other political campaigns over the years until he hooked up with State Senator Richard M. Daley. Daley was about to announce for the office of Cook County Clerk, or so Skinny and others thought. But the powerful alderman and committeeman of the 25th Ward, Vito Marzullo, blocked Daley. A man named Stanley Kusper, who was out of Marzullo's stable, was already the County Clerk. So Daley held a news conference and announced he was running for state's attorney.

This announcement rocked Mayor Jane Byrne back on her heels. She was convinced that Daley was her main opponent and would challenge her bid for reelection. If elected state's attorney, Daley would have investigative power to look for chicanery at City Hall. Let's face it. Anyone can find some chicanery at City Hall if they know where to look.

Mayor Byrne enlisted 14th Ward Alderman Eddie Burke to run against Daley in the Democratic primary. Daley easily defeated Burke in March by a two-to-one margin. Byrne's support didn't help Senator Ted Kennedy's presidential hopes that year. President Jimmy Carter defeated Kennedy in the Illinois primary.

"I was good at getting people to go into different areas and go door to door. It was before all this stuff where you raise millions of dollars and hire some guy like you were selling soap detergent or something and put on all these negative commercials. People would put literature together and go and talk to their neighbors. It was very good. People don't vote today because they don't participate. The process is all about money today. What was fun when Daley ran for state's attorney was that we were the outsiders. We were against the organization. So we had to create our own. We had many people volunteer. We had a lot of policemen and firemen. We had people who wanted to see some sanity brought back to the mayor's office. What was great was everybody in the campaign was a volunteer, nobody *had* to be there.

"I went to work for Daley in the state's attorney's office. I was in this new unit that was a reach-out program to community groups, senior citizens and the schools. And it worked well for me 'cause I came from the schools. I worked with Kathy Osterman, Norm Willis, Eileen Carey and myself. We had our own office. I worked there for three years. In the summer of 1982 we had a meeting in Grand Beach, Michigan, at the Daley summer home. Those in attendance were Senator Jeremiah Joyce, Tim Degnan, Bill Daley, Tom Carey and Frank Kruesi. We had different sessions. We planned the campaign, fundraising, literature. We had a terrific team together.

"They wanted to make a statement, so they went out and got 300 thousand signatures on Daley's petitions for mayor. Nobody had ever gotten that many signatures."[1]

JIM STRICKLIN was one of the first black cameramen to work for NBC News. A native of Syracuse, he came to Chicago in the late 1950s to study photography at the Illinois Institute of Technology. After college, he tried to get into Local 66 of the International Association of Theatrical and Stage Employees Union, which represented film cameramen. Stricklin couldn't get in. He didn't have the right sponsors. There were no African Americans in that union. So he went to work as a still photographer and became interested in animation. Later he heard that a black man might have an easier time in Canada. He knew guys who had trained up there, so he sent a letter with a sample of his work to the National Film Board Academy in Ottawa and soon learned he was accepted.

Stricklin wasn't in Canada very long when restrictions would dog him again. This time the Canadian Parliament passed a law which said only Canadian citizens or those of the British Commonwealth nations could attend the film academy. Fortunately, one of the people at the Film Board helped him get a job at the Canadian Broadcasting Company in Toronto, where he learned to be a newsreel cameraman.

---

1 James "Skinny" Sheahan, interviewed by author, Chicago, IL, October 24, 2006.

"One day I got a call from a producer named Les Crystal who asked if I wanted to come to work for NBC News in Chicago. It was in the early days of the civil rights movement and they needed a black cameraman, somebody who was already trained. There was no affirmative action back then."[2]

Stricklin went to Chicago and met with the news director, Angus "Bill" Corley, a pioneer in diversity hiring at NBC. "I expressed concern about getting into the union," Stricklin said, "but Corley told me, 'I'm hiring you. If I hire you the union has to take you'."[3]

At first the union gave him a hard time, but Stricklin toughed it out. He would work for NBC News for thirty-five years, travel extensively throughout the United States and abroad and photograph some of the important events in the latter half of the twentieth century. One of them was the 1983 election for mayor of Chicago.

VINCE TENUTO *eases the Oldsmobile Cutlass to the curb in front of Rich Daley's home on Emerald Avenue on the near Southwest Side. The young candidate is in his trademark rumpled raincoat.*

Tenuto and Daley drive the better part of an hour to Devon Avenue in the far North Side neighborhood of West Rogers Park. Tenuto parks the car and remains a reasonable distance behind while Daley strolls the thoroughfare. I'm there with a camera crew to record the event. It's where I first meet Vince Tenuto, a jovial fellow, who scolds me about my beat up shoes. These were not the type of shoes he thought were proper for a television man. We watch Daley walk slowly as the cameraman does his thing. He does not have the purposeful walk of his father. And it's tough getting the hand out of the raincoat pocket to offer it to a passerby. He is still as shy as I remember him in the state legislature.

Vince Tenuto is one of those quintessential neighborhood men who can be counted on to get things done, a constant volunteer. Toward the end of World War II, he volunteered for the Marine Corps. The only problem was his age. He was only sixteen and had

---

2   Jim Stricklin, interviewed by author, Chicago, IL, October 24, 2007.
3   Ibid.

forged his papers. When the Marines found out, they gave him an honorable discharge and sent him home.

Vince grew up in a neighborhood called "the Patch" in the vicinity of Chicago and Western Avenues on the West Side. It was mostly Italian and butted up against the old Polish neighborhood immediately to the east.

"We belonged to Holy Rosary parish but I went to the Chopin public school. My mother died in 1945. I worked for the county as a tree trimmer. Later, I became a Park District policeman, and in 1961 I went to work in the Chicago Police Department under Superintendent O.W. Wilson. I left the police force on March 1, 1985. I got connected with Rich Daley in 1980 in his race for Cook County state's attorney. I drove his mother, Mrs. Daley, to many campaign events. I held my first St. Joseph's Table right after the primary election in March of 1980. What I like about Rich is he's not a tyrant. He never talks down to people. The one thing he got from his father and his mother, who I think was a saint, is he never forgot where he came from and where he's going."[4] (St. Joseph's Table, the Italian feast, is still going on today under Vince's sponsorship.)

RUSS EWING was a classic overachiever. An African American who was orphaned as a small boy, he was raised by foster parents on the South Side. Ewing began taking piano lessons at an early age and played jazz for the rest of his life. He played at clubs all over Chicago and once went to the West Coast to work for comedian Bob Hope.

Ewing later joined the Chicago Fire Department where he served for several years, then took all his savings to pay for night school at Northwestern University. He went to New York to write the great American novel but never finished it. He did meet an NBC executive who liked his writing and referred him to Angus "Bill" Corley, a visionary news executive—the same man who had hired cameraman Jim Stricklin. It was the 1960s and television news was a growth industry. Corley had no opening for a writer at

---

4   Vince Tenuto, interviewed by author, Chicago, IL, December 8, 2006.

NBC Chicago but offered Ewing a job as a courier until something opened. He took it. Thus began a legendary career as a Chicago television newsman that lasted nearly forty years.

Soon Ewing was doing stories about how easy it was to buy guns on the streets of Chicago; he would buy the guns himself in back alleys. He would chronicle the plight of prostitutes coming out of morning court. At some point a trademark Ewing story began. A fugitive black man would surrender to Russ and let Russ turn him over to the police. The idea was the suspect might avoid a beating from the cops if they knew Ewing was on the story. It would happen many times over the years, Russ even flying his own small plane with a suspect into Meigs Field just south of downtown as the cameras rolled.

Ewing usually specialized in crime stories, but in the Chicago mayoral election of 1983, a blockbuster political story would come his way.

TOM MANION was a politician's dream. He was single, loved politics and had a great capacity for work. He didn't need a government job and didn't want one. He was a successful salesman and would take time off for political campaigns. He was the son of an IBEW worker and lived in the western suburb of Elmhurst. He got the political bug reading books about the late Mayor Daley and the Democratic Machine, including *Boss* by Mike Royko and *Clout* by Len O'Connor. He also read Professor Milton Rakove's Machine handbooks entitled *Don't Make No Waves...Don't Back No Losers* and *We Don't Want Nobody Nobody Sent*.

Manion went to work for Rich Daley in his campaign for state's attorney in 1980. In the campaign of 1983, Manion was in charge of field operations in nine wards on the North Side, seven along the lakefront, plus the 47th and 40th Wards. With the exception of the 42nd Ward headed by Daley ally George Dunne, the other eight ward organizations were supporting Mayor Byrne. So every day Manion was battling behind enemy lines. One of the toughest battlegrounds was the 47th Ward, which was run by Ed Kelly, a former Marine, who ran the Chicago Park District. He and his organization were solid for Jane Byrne.

S TEVEN FLOWERS will tell you that most of his life he has been an activist in all sorts of things, neighborhood issues, politics; you name it, Steven Flowers was involved. This stemmed from the idea that African Americans were always getting shortchanged when it came to public services and opportunities to pursue the American dream. So Steven Flowers set out to change all of that.

Flowers grew up in the Altgeld Gardens Public Housing project on the far South Side. The fact that his mother looked "white" would cause him and his siblings much trouble in that tough neighborhood. He went to Carver High School and later graduated from Chicago Vocational, where he was an officer in the Army ROTC. There was much more education in his future: Malcolm X College, a degree from Columbia College, fine arts study at Southern Illinois University and a master's degree in social work from Aurora University.

He got married and had a son. Flowers had recalled a brother having trouble with street gangs as a youth, so he took his young family and moved to the other end of the city, the far North Side 49th Ward. There he took a job with the Council for Jewish Elderly. He made many neighborhood contacts. He became a deputy voter registrar for Cook County and registered hundreds of people to vote. He became active in Network 49, one of the independent political organizations on the North Side.

In 1983, Steve Flowers was delighted to find himself working on the campaign of Harold Washington for mayor. He would go door to door, work late at night, conduct literature blitzes, and even get arrested for the cause.

T OM CAREY got interested in politics very early in life. He has vivid memories of the 1960 campaign of John F. Kennedy. He remembers the people coming to vote at three or four precinct polling places in the basement of his church, St. Margaret Queen of Scotland on the South Side. He was in first grade.

At thirteen, he was working on the 1968 presidential campaign of Senator Eugene McCarthy of Minnesota. He ran errands and licked envelopes and remembers being in a television news story with actor Tony Randall. In 1974, he was involved in the campaign of Jeremiah Joyce, who won an aldermanic race against Mayor Daley's chosen candidate.

Later he rang doorbells for Mike Howlett, who beat incumbent Governor Dan Walker in a primary contest in 1976. Carey had worked at the Board of Trade and in the financial markets and had a gift for crunching numbers. He found out early that some of the people running political campaigns knew very little about the study of polling numbers and the proper placement of precinct workers where they might have the most success soliciting votes. Carey estimates that his total earnings from government or political payrolls would not exceed forty thousand dollars. Once he drove a truck to supplement his income. He was not in it for the money.

Carey hooked up with Richard M. Daley in 1979 and managed his countywide precinct organization during Daley's successful run for state's attorney in 1980. Like many Daley admirers, Carey appreciated his low-key style. "There was never any schmaltz with him. He wasn't one of these glad to see you guys. He was very good one on one. You could talk about your problems and you always knew he was trying just as hard as you were."

Tom Carey would run the Daley for Mayor citywide precinct organization in the 1983 primary election.

LINDSLEY "JELLY" HOLT was a precinct captain in the neighborhood around 48th and Calumet in the 3rd Ward on the South Side. In the 1983 mayoral election, he was seventy-two years old and had reached the pinnacle of his career. He claimed never to have lost an election in his precinct. He had started in political work as a Republican when he was only nine years old and changed when South Side boss Bill Dawson led much of the African American community into the Democratic Party.

Jelly Holt was an engaging, bubbly personality. A robust man, as his nickname implied, he had been a drummer in a small band called the Four Blazes that played in clubs all over the city. He was a natural for political work and the Democratic Party rewarded him with the much coveted "spot in the hall." Jelly Holt had a desk job in the Department of Streets and Sanitation answering complaints about garbage service. In his basement rec room were pictures of Jelly with celebrities: Mayor Bilandic and his wife and Alderman Ty Kenner, Teddy Kennedy, and Muhammad Ali.

The 3rd Ward, once dominated by Roy and Harold Washington, was now run by Tyrone Kenner, and Kenner was supporting Jane Byrne. This would be tough on the veteran precinct captain. Jelly believed that if you served your people day in and day out, they would come out and vote for you.

Jelly explained how things had changed in his precinct: "There was a time when you could go in a house and kiss a baby, give a child candy, give the mother a smock or something, and everybody in the house would vote for you. Now, there's TV and radio and another thing both parties don't understand, black people are getting educated. I've always believed in the system. Don't knock the system. Join it. Then you can try to change it."[5]

D AVID AXELROD grew up in New York City. As an adult, he would claim that his love of politics came from a childhood memory of watching John F. Kennedy campaign for the presidency when he was only five years old. Axelrod came west to the University of Chicago, where he studied political science and had a part time job as a reporter for the *Hyde Park Herald*, the neighborhood newspaper near the university. Later he landed an internship with the *Chicago Tribune*, which promptly hired him when he graduated in 1977. He was twenty-one years old.

Axelrod plunged into the job, becoming one of the paper's most prolific political writers. He covered many political meetings in the black neighborhoods of the South Side and was deeply involved in the 1977 special election for mayor. Harold Washington would become the candidate of the African American community but lost

---

5   Lindsley "Jelly" Holt, interviewed by author, Chicago, IL, January 27, 1984.

to Michael Bilandic. Occasionally he shared a byline with F. Richard Ciccone, the *Tribune's* political editor, or William Griffin, later to become Mayor Jane Byrne's chief of staff.

By the time of the 1983 mayoral campaign, David Axelrod was a seasoned veteran of political reporting. He would be everywhere during that campaign and witness some of its most controversial events. He was aggressive and tough. He must have rubbed Mayor Byrne the wrong way because at a campaign news conference, when he asked a rather routine question, the mayor sniped, "David, if I respected you I'd answer. But I don't respect you so I won't answer."

I AM SENT ON ASSIGNMENT *to interview Renault Robinson. I have seen the man before several times when he was organizing black cops and annoying the department brass with demands for better opportunities for minority officers. On this day the story is that Renault is being punished for his activities. I'm sent to meet him in an alley behind the police headquarters at Eleventh and State Streets. It's a blizzardy winter day and through the snow I can make out a lone figure halfway down the alley. He's in uniform with a heavy winter overcoat and a hat with ear flaps. There's nothing in the alley but accumulating snow. "What are you doing here, Renault?" "This is my new beat," he says. "But there's nothing here." "Well, you know how it is, Pete."*

Renault Robinson was a native South Sider and graduate of Hyde Park High School who joined the Chicago Police Department in the early 1960s. At the time, Chicago was slow in getting African Americans on the force. A few blacks held ranking positions in the department, but they were handpicked by their Irish superiors for their willingness to follow orders. Usually these men were Catholic.

During the turbulent '60s, Robinson and other black officers became concerned about police brutality, especially during rioting which followed the murder of Dr. Martin Luther King, Jr. They formed the Afro American Patrolmen's League, which focused attention on racial issues within the department. The League was a constant aggravation to the police department and the administration of Richard J. Daley. One year, Robinson's group was successful in getting the federal government to withhold $95 million in federal funds for the department because of discriminatory hiring and promotion practices. And the League joined a successful lawsuit against the city, which resulted in major changes in how the department hired and promoted women and minorities. Mayor Richard J. Daley abhorred what he referred to as racial quotas. The *Chicago Tribune* called Renault Robinson Daley's number one enemy. All the while, Renault Robinson was in constant trouble with his superiors, sometimes getting arrested. He gave as good as he got, once calling on the superintendant of police to resign. Eventually Robinson left the police department, but he remained an activist in Chicago's African American community.

In 1977, Robinson was working on Harold Washington's first run for mayor. They had an office on Seventy-First Street and the campaign was being run by Gus Savage, publisher of community newspapers and later to become a congressman. For the first time, Robinson had exposure to a citywide campaign. Alliances were made in some of the white communities. He learned a lot about structure and logistics. Blacks had not had this type of experience before, their political activities being confined to the African American neighborhoods on the South and West Sides. Robinson and his campaign workers learned some things about the Polish American community, Italian Americans and the Jewish community along the lakefront. As he recalled many years later, "We had people going out into these white communities at a time when it wasn't very cozy for a black person to do. But there was always somebody who was sympathetic, who thought this was a good thing."[6]

In 1977, while the Washington campaign was reaching out for meager support in the white community, Renault Robinson and others found they had plenty of work to do convincing the African American community that a black could get elected mayor of Chicago. The prevailing view was that Harold Washington and his supporters were wasting their time. By the time Harold Washington

---

6 Renault Robinson, interviewed by author, Chicago, IL, June 24, 2009.

ran again in 1983, Renault Robinson had learned how to counter that mindset.

When Jane Byrne scored her stunning upset of the Machine in 1979, she occasionally called Renault Robinson to get advice on issues important to the African American community. In June of that year, she appointed him to the board of the Chicago Housing Authority. But within six months, the controversial Robinson was saying that Byrne would be a one-term mayor, that she had broken most of her promises and was associating with unsavory Machine hacks.

Robinson was on the platform when Harold Washington announced for mayor. He would become the manager of the campaign.

★ CHAPTER 8 ★

The Primary

AFTER RICHARD M. DALEY was elected state's attorney and the administration of Mayor Jane M. Byrne continued to mire itself in controversy, Daley was frequently asked if he would challenge the mayor's bid for reelection. His pat standard answer was, "I have no intentions." This was a cute little twist on the usual response politicians give when asked if they are using their current office as a stepping stone to something bigger. "This is the job I want. I'm not interested in governor or senator; I'm focused on this job." The media and the general public are aware of this little charade. They know the real answer for most politicians is, "If I get a chance for some better office, I'll grab it." Daley was no different than most others. Polls showed him a favorite over Byrne and suddenly he had intentions.

On November 4, 1982, more than one hundred well wishers and representatives of the news media gathered in a ballroom of the Midland Hotel in downtown Chicago. Forty-year-old Richard M. Daley was surrounded by family as he approached the podium for a long-expected announcement that he was indeed a candidate for mayor of Chicago. Daley had been taking speech lessons from a professor at Northwestern University. He made his prepared statement with barely a flaw. He accused Mayor Jane Byrne of mismanagement. People were worried about Chicago's future. It was time for leadership. That would be the theme of the Daley campaign. Brother William would be the campaign manager. A top flight *Tribune* reporter, Bob Benjamin, was named press secretary.

After the news conference, Daley made appearances in ethnic neighborhoods throughout the city. He accused Byrne of raising taxes and fees by more than $400 million and causing chaos in city government by her frequent firings and hirings. She had made a mess of the school system and public housing. He made seven well orchestrated stops, telling black ministers on the West Side that Byrne had failed to criticize the policies of Republican President Ronald Reagan and Governor James Thompson. He ended the day walking and shaking hands on State Street and in the Daley Center Plaza.

Before the primary campaign of 1983, there was considerable talk in political circles and around City Hall that Jane Byrne wanted to get a black candidate into the race. She and her advisors believed her main challenger was Daley. The idea was that a third, African American candidate would take votes from Daley because Byrne had angered black voters. The rumor persists to this day that a couple of top Machine guys delivered a large chunk of cash to Harold to help get his campaign started.

From the very beginning, Harold Washington was the overwhelming choice of Chicago's African American community to be its standard bearer in the race for mayor. Lu Palmer, a former *Daily News* reporter and community activist, had organized a coalition of black community organizations and begun a draft Washington movement in July. Washington had been reluctant all the way. He wanted assurances of full support from the community, a healthy campaign war chest and a black voter registration drive. There were other qualified black candidates, including state Comptroller Roland Burris. But despite some rough spots in his history, Harold was the choice of his people. The math was enticing. Daley and Byrne would divide the white vote. Alderman Roman Pucinski was considered a possible third white candidate who would siphon even more votes from the Northwest Side. Even with only 70% of the African American vote, a black candidate had a real chance of winning. And there were 100,000 new black voters on the rolls.

On November 10 at the Hyde Park Hilton Hotel, Harold Washington announced that he would seek the Democratic nomination for mayor of Chicago. His fiancée and long time companion, Mary

Ella Smith, joined him. Washington declared that the city that works doesn't work anymore and Chicago was a city in decline. Although some white elected officials were on hand, the majority of the crowd was black. Washington said his jailing for failure to file tax returns was behind him and his life was an open book.

Renault Robinson, head of the African American Police Organization, was named the campaign manager. Robinson had played a key role in securing radio advertising for the black voter registration drive. Pat Caddell, who gained fame as President Jimmy Carter's pollster, joined the Washington team. Bill Zimmerman was the media consultant. Lu Palmer, who engineered Washington's candidacy, called the campaign a crusade. He said he felt a religious fervor out in the community.

On November 22, Mayor Jane Byrne held a news conference on the fifth floor of City Hall to announce that she was a candidate for reelection. Daughter Kathy and husband Jay McMullen were at her side. Her main message was that she had inherited a city that was in dire financial straits and that she had managed to turn it all around. She said the tough times were over now and she had absolutely no intention of raising taxes in the future.

City Hall observers noticed a brand new Jane Byrne. She had a new wardrobe, a new air of confidence. She looked like a chief executive who was in complete charge. Her New York media consultants had done a magnificent job. She had a campaign war chest in the millions. The next day, she would receive the formal endorsement of the Cook County Democratic Party. It was all pretty heady for a woman who, just four years ago, had been campaigning in a wig.

Early research by media people showed that the Chicago electorate was angry and disappointed in Mayor Byrne, even wanted her out of office. But it also showed that the voters saw her as powerful, and Chicagoans respect power. So the media advisors began crafting a plan to use that perception of power in Byrne's favor.

Despite all his difficulties with her in the past, William Griffin came back to manage Jane Byrne's reelection campaign. One of his first tasks was to hire a media consultant. Griffin picked David Sawyer of New York.

A graduate of Princeton, Sawyer was one of the pioneer political gurus who emerged in the 1970s and used sophisticated polling and focus groups to measure the feelings of voters. A former Israeli intelligence officer who was also a psychiatrist handled research for the firm. Sawyer had worked in presidential politics and done campaigns in Israel and South America. He had an engaging personality and connected immediately with the often difficult Jane Byrne.

On November 30, 1982, the city's Republican ward committeemen gathered to select a candidate for mayor. Less than half the fifty wards were represented, indicating a lack of interest in a candidate who was probably going nowhere. Still the committee plowed ahead and unanimously endorsed sixty-one-year-old Bernard Epton, a lawyer and veteran of fourteen years in the Illinois House. His name was not well-known outside of legislative circles. But Epton vowed to raise a half million dollars, wage a vigorous campaign and rebuild the GOP in Chicago. "If the Democrats keep on fighting and don't make up," Epton prophesied, "who knows what might happen after the primary."

The committee had earlier screened four other candidates, including a businessman, a city planner, a college professor and a salesman who was also a part time performer called Spanky the Clown.

After his announcement and party endorsement, Epton would have a difficult time getting attention for the next few months. President Reagan came to town to attend a fundraiser for Senator Charles Percy. Bernie Epton was seated near the back of the room and was never introduced. He had to buy his own ticket. This was the way Chicago regarded Republican candidates for mayor.

The Democratic primary campaign for mayor began slowly. Late November and December was the holiday season. The public and the news media were captivated by a still unresolved election for governor of Illinois. Incumbent James R. Thompson clung to a five thousand vote lead over Senator Adlai Stevenson out of more than three and a half million votes cast. Stevenson's camp found widespread voting irregularities and asked the Illinois Supreme Court to order a recount. Thompson was opposed. The court had a four-to-three Democratic majority. But, just before the scheduled inauguration, it ruled in favor of Thompson. The swing vote was Democrat Seymour Simon, a former Chicago alderman, who sided with the Republicans. Election analysts took note of the huge African American vote for Stevenson in the city of Chicago.

The Byrne camp was not idle over the holidays. A wave of television commercials hit the airwaves. Jane Byrne was portrayed now as an experienced manager, a powerful business woman running a city that was confronting very difficult financial problems.

The Daley campaign was caught off guard. Manager Bill Daley didn't think he could compete with the Byrne money machine. He was going to hold off on the media buy until the end of the campaign. And it was tough raising money. Daley's people believed that Mayor Byrne and Chairman Vrdolyak were doing a pretty good job of blocking big contributors to the Daley campaign. Daley did have a valuable ally in the prominent Pritzker family. They owned the Hyatt Hotel chain and Daley had use of the Hyatt downtown for fundraisers, news conferences and other campaign events.

During the holidays it was still seen as a Byrne-Daley contest, with Daley holding a lead in most of the polls. But the Byrne television ads were making a dent. And some of the political wise guys were still worried about the big increases in African American voter registrations. In late September, the Chicago Board of Elections had reported that a coalition of community organizations called POWER helped register thirty thousand new voters. Eighty percent of them were African American. By the time of the primary election, the number of new African American voters was estimated at one hundred thousand. The Chicago Board of Elections reported that more than a million and a half people were registered and eligible to vote in the primary election. The new enrollees in the black community had voted heavily for Adlai Stevenson for governor in November. Would they unite behind Harold in the election for mayor? The smart money was betting the Machine would still control a good portion of the black vote for Byrne. Washington would close Daley out of the black community.

The Daley-Byrne brawl was a street reporter's dream, something happening all the time out in the neighborhoods. The big time news people rarely saw any of this, content to headquarter in the City Hall press room and shuttle to selected campaign events.

A schism was happening in the 47th Ward on the North Side around the old Lincoln Avenue German neighborhood. The ward boss was Ed Kelly, a tough former boxer and World War II Marine veteran. Kelly was the president of the Chicago Park District and had thousands of jobs under his control, many of which went to his loyal precinct workers and their relatives. This made the 47th one of the strongest Democratic wards in the city. Kelly, once considered an heir apparent to Mayor Richard J. Daley, was a solid supporter of Mayor Byrne.

The Daley people had infiltrated Kelly territory, signing up many volunteers, including some of Kelly's top precinct captains. One of them was Horace Lindsey, the ward secretary and superintendant of employment at the park district. When it was discovered that Lindsey and his family had contributed to the Daley campaign, he was fired from both his jobs. In late November of 1982, Lindsey filed suit in federal court, claiming he was fired from the park district because of his support for Daley, a violation of the federal Shakman decree which prohibited hiring and firing for political reasons. Among other things, Lindsey charged that Mayor Byrne had warned him about supporting Daley. He also claimed that Cook County Democratic Chairman Ed Vrdolyak told him to get in line and go to Kelly on bended knee. Vrdolyak denied the allegation.

Thomas Allen, ward superintendant in charge of city services in the 47th, boldly opened a Daley for Mayor headquarters on Lincoln Ave. The 47th Ward, sometimes called the Fighting 47th, was shaping up to be a major battleground.

Tom Manion was a Daley campaign coordinator for the North Side wards, including the 47th. As Manion said, "We had an office on Lincoln Avenue run by Lindsey, Tommy Allen, the ward superintendent, and Blackie Madison. These guys worked like dogs. Every night after closing the office they'd go out drinking until the bars closed. Then they'd have fist fights with Kelly's people. Kelly's people would throw bricks through our windows and we'd throw bricks through their windows. Then we were throwing bricks through our own windows 'cause we were trying to get media attention. And it was really crazy with all the drinking and all that. Horace was in the 17th Precinct near Irving and Western. He had a coffee in his house for Mrs. Daley. Bill Daley knew about all the fighting in the 47th and he called to tell me to make sure everything was OK up there 'cause his mother was going to an event at Lindsey's. So I went over and noticed that Lindsey had men posted on every street corner in the neighborhood. This was before cell phones and I wanted to make sure everything was jake 'cause Mrs. Daley was making an appearance in Lindsey's basement. The 4th Precinct captain of the 47th Ward was Tony Teramino. He had one hundred park district jobs in his one precinct. He also had his own snow plow and would plow the sidewalks of his people. He gave turkeys away at Thanksgiving. That's what we were up against in the 47th."[1]

On the South Side, Skinny Sheahan was running the Daley operation in the 13th Ward. They had a real dump of a campaign office next to a VFW Hall. Volunteers were putting up Daley signs everywhere. "Once a week we'd put a big Daley sign on Mike Madigan's lawn. He'd go absolutely crazy." (Mayor Byrne had gotten Madigan's attention early on when she fired one of his top precinct captains from a big job in Streets and Sanitation.) "Occasionally fights would break out between our people and his over the signs." "Were the police called?" Skinny was asked. "The cops were involved in a lot of the fighting. They were our cops, volunteers."[2]

According to Sheahan, the Daley people were knocking on doors every day in the 13th Ward. There might be 425 people on a precinct polling sheet. The workers got to know every one of them. They came to know the names of the husband and wife and the kids, even the dog. The job was to identify the people who were for Daley and make sure they came out on Election Day. They found a lot of support for Richard M. Daley in the 13th Ward, many people fondly remembering his father.

1 Tom Manion, interviewed by author, Rosemont, IL, October 3, 2007.
2 James "Skinny" Sheahan, interview.

The great thing about the campaign, according to Skinny Sheahan, was that none of Daley's people had to be there. No one was protecting a job. No one was getting paid a penny. "We had a nurse from Children's Memorial Hospital come in one day and she wanted to volunteer. I asked her why and she said that Daley had been the best parent she ever saw at the hospital. When his son Kevin was sick he came every night unannounced and stayed all night with his son. She worked one of the precincts for us in the 13th Ward."[3]

The three candidates for the Democratic nomination for mayor of Chicago engaged in four debates during the last two weeks of January.

The first encounter was broadcast live in prime time on four local television stations. It was sponsored by the *Chicago Sun Times* and the moderator was the paper's handsome, young, hard charging publisher, James Hoge. The topic was city finances. The people questioning the candidates were Elinor Elam of the League of Women Voters, Carol Marin of WMAQ-TV, Robert Jordan of WGN-TV and Basil Talbot, Jr., political editor of the *Sun Times*. Absent for some unexplained reason was Harry Golden, Jr., the veteran *Sun Times* City Hall reporter and an expert on the municipal budget. Perhaps the flamboyant Golden, a throwback to the front page era of journalism, was not buttoned down enough for this group.

Byrne stood on a small platform throughout to be equal in height to her opponents. She never flinched as Washington opened with a charge that she was destroying the city. He said Chicago was threatened by a fiscal time bomb set to go off right after the primary. Dressed in a gorgeous cream-colored suit, this was the new Jane Byrne, who had rescued the city from the brink of financial disaster and was now moving forward. She charged that the New York bond rating agencies had been lied to by previous administrations about the city and school board's woeful financial condition. The news media, sometimes unfairly, had painted Byrne as a crazy lady, hiring and firing on a whim. The *Sun Times* had even done a feature article trying to psychoanalyze the first woman mayor. But

---

3 James "Skinny" Sheahan, interview.

the Jane Byrne of the first debate appeared to be a cool, seasoned executive who knew how to wield power.

The first debate was golden for Harold Washington. First of all, he looked the part. Those who knew him best were probably surprised. He appeared in a beautiful blue-gray three piece suit. Throughout his career, Washington was known for a somewhat disheveled look, tie and collar askew, partially shaven. This night, he was immaculately groomed. And his command of the language was spectacular. He used words like "assiduously" when he described how he would cut fat from every city department. He would also take a meat cleaver to "burgeoning" city consulting fees. Washington was willing to support an increase in the income tax if the city could get more funding from the state. He also favored a hike in utility taxes. Both Byrne and Daley opposed any new taxes but, under sharp questioning from the panel, neither had any hard answers on how to solve the city's budget shortfalls.

Harold Washington was a big hit in the African American community. As Renault Robinson would later point out, many black Chicagoans were skeptical about Washington's candidacy. They had seen it before. Another black candidate headed for the also ran column. But Congressman Washington appeared to be different. He was an exciting personality who looked like he could handle the two front runners who were fracturing the white vote.

Even Richard M. Daley, the least gifted speaker of the three, could find a few highlights in that first debate. His supporters were pleased that he didn't have any major screw-ups. At age forty-one, he was the most youthful looking of the three candidates. But at times his statements seemed to ramble. "We have been dealing with the CTA, the failure of this administration so you have $30 million for the CTA which it failed to get." Maybe it wasn't quite clear, but Daley delivered with authority and it sounded good. When he would finish one of those hazy statements, his eyes would dart away, almost like he was saying, "Did anybody understand what I just said?"

Richard M. Daley, like his father, did not have a flare for public speaking. Years before, his father had received professional help from a speech professor at Northwestern University. There was deep concern about young Daley's ability to perform in televised debates, which were certain to come in the campaign. So a Northwestern professor was hired. His name was Irving Rein, a specialist in speech and communications.

Rein and Daley began rigorous practice sessions. Daley would read speeches and answer questions in front of the camera. Then they would play it back and Rein would offer his instruction. Rein would recall years later that Daley was a tough and instinctual politician, and he felt it was his job to make him an effective communicator. But Daley's attention span was short. He did not take suggestions well and he was uncomfortable with the sessions. At times he would grow frustrated and just walk out of the office for a half hour.[4]

The Daley camp was worried about the debates. Everyone knew this was not his long suit. At one point there was even talk of giving him an earpiece with a radio transmitter so he could be coached live on the air. Wisely, that idea was dropped.

In subsequent debates, Washington charged that Chicago was the organized crime capital of the world and that Byrne had institutionalized racism in the city. Daley attacked Byrne's new Madison Avenue image. But Byrne was unflappable. She was a very attractive lady with blonde hair and a trim figure. But she always had trouble smiling. Her look was always that of a strict nun who had just caught some boys smoking behind the school. It was a very severe look. Nevertheless, Byrne and Harold Washington seemed to get the most points in the debates.

In all four debates, neither Byrne nor Daley ever mentioned Harold Washington's conviction for failing to file income tax returns and the suspension of his law license for failing to provide service to clients. It was still thought of as a Byrne-Daley battle. That would change abruptly.

On January 24, the *Chicago Sun Times* and WMAQ-TV came out with a poll showing Mayor Byrne with a commanding 20 point

---

4   Professor Irving Rein, "The Transformation of a Candidate: Richard M. Daley," *American Communication Journal,* January 2000.

lead over Washington, and Daley running third. It was a low point for the Daley campaign.

You can't have an election in Chicago without a scandal coming to the attention of the public.

Every true Chicagoan knows that the fix is always in. Nothing is on the square. And if you don't have any clout, you've got nothing. And this is how it goes. An average mope appears at the auto pound with his hat in hand. And some tough guy from the 11th Ward is sneering at him from behind the counter and treating him like a dog. And he gives the guy the hundred bucks to get his car and all the while he's thinking this imbecile, who couldn't handle a real job, could at least smile as he takes my money. But in Chicago, only a sucker beefs. So he keeps his mouth shut.

Yet every so often the stars arrange in a certain way over the city. And the clout heavy wise guys and the fixers get their just due. It's called the federal investigation. Young, well scrubbed, buttoned down federal agents and assistant U.S. attorneys fan out across the city looking for squealers. The news media views the feds as infallible, which they aren't. But many times they do get it right and they ferret out the bad guys. That tough guy who's been lording it over everybody is seen being led away in handcuffs. And that big shot from City Hall is hiding his face from the camera, revealing the shiny, freshly manicured fingernails. And from the cars on the crowded expressway and the buses and El trains, you can almost hear the muffled hurrah coming from behind the newspaper. Yeah, yeah. They got those bastards!

Sometimes, the federal probe gets clouded by politics. Since everybody's squealing on everybody else, the feds, on occasion, rely on the wrong squealer.

In the Democratic primary campaign for mayor of Chicago in 1983 there was such a federal investigation. How much impact it had on the outcome of the contest is still debated. It had all of the ingredients of a bona fide Chicago political scandal. Officials of the Continental Air Transport Company found themselves in a nasty situation in 1982. The company had an exclusive franchise to operate buses from O'Hare Airport to downtown Chicago hotels. It was a good, profitable business, but it depended solely on periodic approval by the Chicago City Council. Continental was owned by Checker Motors Corporation of Kalamazoo, Michigan, which also operated the two dominant taxi cab companies in Chicago. Checker Motors got the word that Mayor Byrne opposed the company having a monopoly on public transportation to and from O'Hare. And the City Council had been sitting on the company's request for an extension of its contract for over a year.

So Checker Motors Corporation did the right thing. In December, it sold the bus company to a group of Chicagoans headed by Thomas Meagher for $4.4 million. Meagher, a politically well connected Chicagoan, had been the president of Continental Air Transport. As soon as that contract was complete, the City Council did the right thing. It extended Continental's exclusive franchise to provide bus service from O'Hare. This all might have slipped by quietly like other Chicago political-business transactions, except for the heated primary election now underway in early 1983.

New details about the sale of Continental came out in the papers. An attorney for the parent Checker Motors said the company was all but forced to sell the bus business. He had been told that Bill Griffin and Mike Brady, two of the mayor's former aides, were part of the group doing the buying. Brady and Griffin now had their own consulting company and obviously reached an accord with the mayor. The new firm had received some city business and Griffin was now Byrne's campaign manager. Byrne had also appointed Griffin to a spot on the Regional Transportation Authority board and Brady to the board of the Chicago Transit Authority.

Griffin denied ever considering an investment in Continental, although he said he did receive a $3000 fee to help with Continental's presentation to the City Council. Speaking for his partner, Brady, he said Brady had once considered joining the new buyers but lacked sufficient funds. The name of Charlie Swibel, the real estate mogul, advisor and chief fundraiser for Byrne, also figured prominently in the stories. He allegedly warned Checker to sell or lose their O'Hare bus routes. Meantime, Checker officials said they had other potential buyers who dropped out when they saw the Chicago style writing on the wall.

There was a flurry of activity. Independent aldermen called for a City Council investigation. So did State's Attorney Daley, although he said he would entrust the job to a top assistant. And, of course, the feds said they would look into the matter. In the final measurement of such events, nobody went to jail. And the primary campaign ground on.

Volunteers from the Daley campaign turned up some interesting information when they did a random survey of registered voters in five wards. The sampling, which included half the precincts in each ward, showed six thousand voters registered to addresses that were boarded up homes or abandoned buildings. Sixteen people were registered at a McDonald's restaurant, one person in the middle of a park. Daley's legal committee said it had purged most of these people from the rolls and turned its information over to the feds.

While the media and white Chicago still saw it as a Byrne-Daley contest, something was happening in Chicago's African American community. It was like a fire had been lit. Harold Washington had caught fire.

On a Sunday night in early February, I'm sent to the new University of Illinois Pavilion just south of the Loop. The crowd is estimated at twelve thousand. They are predominantly black, from independent South and West Side organizations for Harold. But here and there are scattered some Hispanics and a few whites. It's like a revival meeting. You can feel the fervor. The crowd sits for nearly four hours listening to speeches. Few, if any, leave the building. The stage is filled with prominent black religious, business and political leaders. Members of the congressional black caucus have come to town to show their support. Senator Alan Cranston of California, an announced candidate for president, endorses Harold.

The audience is delighted when Congressman Washington finally takes the stage, chanting, "Har-OLD, Har-OLD." "You want Harold," Washington proclaims, "you got him!" He proceeds to attack Byrne as a flunky for Ronald Reagan and takes a shot at Daley, saying he doesn't have the divine right of kings just because his name is Daley.

"Where we come from you have to work for what you get. You have a right to more than choosing between Tweedledee and Tweedledum." I recall what Harold has said recently: "If anybody doesn't think I can win, they can't count."

Chicago's two major newspapers endorsed Daley, first the *Tribune* toward the end of January and ten days later, the *Sun Times*. Both endorsements seemed to be more of an attack on the wild four years Jane Byrne had given Chicago. Washington was seen as running a racially charged campaign.

The campaign rolled on.

It was a cold night in February and Steve Flowers and his street crew were making the rounds late at night, putting up Washington signs, dropping leaflets in apartment buildings. They called it a literature blitz. Sometimes they would take the signs of opponents down. He saw nothing wrong in it because workers for the Department of Streets and Sanitation were doing the same thing in the daytime. The 49th Ward, the home of Loyola University, was a cosmopolitan place with some diversification. But in 1983, it was still predominantly white and an African American man wandering about late at night might attract attention, especially one who was carrying a bucket of wheat paste to put up signs. Sure enough, the police showed up, plain clothes tactical officers.

Steven Flowers had once worked for the Chicago Transit Authority as a motorman. He still had some of his tools and skeleton keys in his car. They were stamped "Property of the CTA." Flowers would not talk to the police. He felt he had done nothing wrong. The police finally charged him with theft of property for possessing the CTA tools. He had to spend the night in jail. The charges were later dismissed in court.

Although he was the odds-on favorite before the campaign began, Richard M. Daley never did lead in any of the polls taken during the campaign by the media and other candidates. But his own polls were a different story. Daley had the 11th Ward straw poll, which had proved very reliable for his father's organization over the years. It was done very simply. Volunteers went out to shopping centers and other public places around the city with little wooden ballot boxes.

And they asked people to mark ballots. It was similar to the old *Sun Times* straw poll, which many veteran journalists still swear by.

The Daley poll taken the last two weeks of January and first week of February showed gradual progress. January 23 it had Byrne leading by five points, with Washington close behind. One week later, Daley had narrowed the gap to one point, with Washington still very much in the running. The weekend of February 6, Daley took the lead with 30%, Byrne 28% and Harold 27%, a virtual dead heat. This straw poll was taken at fifteen locations throughout the city with 2250 straw ballots taken each weekend. It was the same poll that showed Byrne and Bilandic in a dead heat four years earlier. This same poll showed Daley getting only 8% of the African American vote.

On February 15, former Vice President Walter Mondale came to town and endorsed Daley. Mondale was about to announce his candidacy for President against incumbent Ronald Reagan in 1984. Mondale spent six hours with Daley, appearing at a luncheon of Women for Daley in the Palmer House and later on the Northwest Side, where Committeeman Tommy Lyons predicted Daley would carry his ward by five thousand votes. Finally, the former vice president sang Daley's praises at the Midland Hotel where a thousand cheering young professional people had gathered. Typical of Daley, he did not return the favor and endorse Mondale for president.

In February, the Byrne campaign began to realize that the real threat to her reelection was not Daley, but Harold Washington. She was advised to change her schedule in the closing days of the campaign and try to recover some support in the black community.

About a week before the election, Big Ed Quigley of the 27th Ward held his traditional pre-election rally of campaign workers. Quigley was an old powerhouse. As Commissioner of Sewers, he held many patronage jobs. Quigley was Irish but most of his precinct workers were black. He was getting older; he dated back to the old Mayor Daley and the Roosevelt era. He probably didn't notice that, at this rally for incumbent Mayor Jane Byrne, many of the workers were wearing the blue Washington campaign button. It was a badge of honor in the African American community.

Cook County Democratic Chairman Edward Vrdolyak spoke at a rally of precinct captains on the Northwest Side. It was held in the cafeteria of an insurance company and reporters were not allowed in. But several of them, including the *Tribune's* David Axelrod, hung around outside and could hear Vrdolyak's remarks. He explained to the captains that Harold Washington was now gaining on Mayor Byrne and the Daley candidacy was taking votes away from the mayor. "It's a racial thing," he told them. "It's about keeping the city the way you know it." Vrdolyak would deny making such racially charged comments.

Meanwhile, state Representative Al Ronan, who handled the citywide precinct organization for Byrne, had some powerful get out the vote phone banks working that weekend. They hit hard on the theme "a vote for Daley is a vote for Washington".

The campaign rumbles to its final days. No one seems to have a handle on what the outcome will be. Harold Washington's people are predicting Washington with 37% of the vote, followed by Byrne with 34% and Daley with 29 or 30%. Byrne's managers are saying she will win by forty thousand votes, with Daley second and Washington third. The Daley people are predicting who else but Daley by thirty thousand votes. But it's one of those wonderful elections that comes down to the wire and nobody has an inkling of who will win.

Steve Brown was the press spokesperson and scheduler for the Byrne campaign. He worked under Bill Griffin, the campaign manager. Both were former newspapermen. "On a weekly basis Griffin and I would meet with national political writers: Jack Germond, David Broder and Jules Witcover. They'd want to come in 'cause there was nothing going on nationally. And you had this feisty woman and the son of the late mayor and a black congressman in this race. And I think Griffin and I suggested it was not out of the realm of possibility that Harold Washington could win the primary. And these guys thought we were insane. They said to a man, 'That'll never happen. A black won't be elected mayor of Chicago.' They thought it was all Jane and Rich. I think going into Election Day we had a sense that Harold had a very good chance to win. And I don't think the media ever picked that up."[5]

Tom Carey, a southsider and somewhat of a mad genius at crunching political numbers, was in charge of the citywide precinct organization for Daley. At the end of the campaign, he saw something in various polling numbers he didn't like. Byrne seemed to be taking votes away from Daley because of the successful "a vote for Daley is a vote for Harold" campaign.

He expressed his fears to campaign manager Bill Daley and came up with an ingenious proposal. Why not mount a write-in campaign for Richard M. Daley in the Republican primary race? This would assure Daley a place on the general election ballot in April no matter who won the Democratic primary. It could be done easily on short notice in just the 11th and 19th Wards. Only twelve to fifteen thousand GOP write-in ballots would be needed for Daley to win that primary. (Epton eventually won the Republican primary with just over eleven thousand votes.)

The Daleys passed on the idea.

Election eve, Jane Byrne was out in the neighborhoods. A woman in the crowd shouted out, "Hey Janie, vote for Richie!" Byrne tried to ignore her as she continued shaking hands. The woman persisted, "Hey Janie, vote for Richie!" An irritated Byrne turned and deadpanned, "Well, I'm busy right now." That night, she appeared in a TV commercial: "Fighting off political attacks is nothing compared to fighting to keep this city alive. It's a tough job but I love it and you better believe I'm going to fight to keep it."

Congressman Washington appeared at an Operation Push rally: "We've whipped them to their knees. This city will never be the same again." Earlier at the Cabrini Green Housing complex, he was asked about Vrdolyak's alleged racial comments at a precinct captains meeting: "He's resorted to the last tactic of a scoundrel. He's raised the race card. He may impale himself on his own petard." Holding a microphone and looking up to the faces of public housing residents who had come to their windows, Washington proclaimed, "Punch nine, nine is mine." The audience was delighted.

---

5   Steve Brown, interviewed by author, Washington, IL, April 2, 2007.

Daley had a cheeseburger at lunch with his wife and some campaign aides in Old Town. Later he campaigned at the 63rd Street mall, a black neighborhood on the South Side. Then he ventured into the 10th Ward, Ed Vrdolyak territory.

The Republican candidate was also out the day before the primary election. A photo would appear in *People* Magazine showing Bernard Epton standing all alone on an El platform, holding a campaign sign. The magazine said the man had been ignored for three months. Bernie looked lonely and discouraged. The caption on the photo said a fan had approached Epton and told him, "Your qualifications are wrong. You're honest and smart and Republican."

At night, there was the typical banter on the television news shows. Sports columnist Bill Gleason, a devout southsider, called it for Daley with Washington second and Byrne running third: "But I'd love to see a runoff. Can't we keep this thing going at least until baseball season starts?"

David Axelrod, the young, serious reporter for the *Tribune,* told Channel 5 viewers the race was too close to call but he thought Mayor Byrne had a slight edge.

Psychic Irene Hughes predicted Byrne the winner.

The polling places would be open from 6 AM until 7 PM on Election Day. They would be monitored by thousands of lawyers, state's attorneys, federal agents, policemen and other assorted poll watchers in what would be the most scrutinized election in Chicago's history.

At 9:30 AM on Election Day, Richard M. Daley and wife Maggie walked down Emerald Ave. to vote at their polling place a half block from their home. At that time, turnout seemed to be light, but the precinct captain was not concerned. He had done his job and this neighborhood would turn out big for Daley.

Out in the 13th Ward, Skinny Sheahan was making sure all the Daley people came out to vote. "It meant contacting them by phone or in person the night before. A little reminder card was hung on the door knobs. We had 480 workers in the 13th Ward on Election Day," said Skinny. "All were volunteers. We had a list of all the polling places in the ward. Many of them were in private homes. Can you believe that? You might be voting in a precinct captain's home. So very early on Election Day we'd call up different polling places and say something like, 'This is Federal Agent Harris. We've got a man headed over there, Agent McCarthy, could you have him call his office when he arrives?' We'd do that early before the polls opened 'cause that's when they'd do their shit with the machines, before and after the polls close.

"Shortly before the election I was one hundred percent sure we'd win by three-to-one. I wouldn't say it publicly. I'd tell everybody we were going to win two-to-one. We had done straw polls. Those are the best polls. And they showed us with 75% of the vote."[6]

Skinny Sheahan believed that Ed Vrdolyak's comment to the precinct captains, "a vote for Daley is a vote for Washington", seriously damaged the Daley campaign in the 13th Ward and elsewhere on the Southwest and Northwest Sides. "He was so smart," Skinny said, "he kept denying it to the media and they kept playing it over and over."[7]

Daley did win the primary in the 13th Ward, but only by 54% to 46% over Jane Byrne.

The voter turnout in Chicago was huge, bigger than any primary election turnout since Daley's father ran the first time in 1955. Eighty percent of the city's voters came out, nearly 1.3 million people. The city's African American wards rolled up huge pluralities for Congressman Harold Washington.

---

6 James "Skinny" Sheahan, interview.
7 Ibid.

✳ CHAPTER 9 ✳

Election Night

ELECTION NIGHT is an emotional time for the participants in a tight political campaign. For months, everyone has been going eighty miles an hour and suddenly it's over. You're out of gas and there's nothing more you can do. Years after the election of 1983, Steve Brown of the Byrne campaign recalled his feelings: "Election night, that's when I learned heartbreak. I had done campaign work in college and high school. I thought we had a good chance to win. I thought she had matured. I hadn't given a thought to the idea that if we lose, you're out of work. We didn't declare defeat election night. The next day I helped write the statement that she read."[1]

Tom Carey could see the defeat coming ahead of time. Early on election night, he called Hanke Gratteau, a *Tribune* reporter who worked closely with columnist Mike Royko. Royko was giving election analysis on television. "Tell Mike not to make a fool of himself," he told Gratteau. "Daley is going to come in third." Later, Carey went to an empty office and drank a quart of whiskey by himself.

William Griffin, Byrne's campaign manager, remembered that last night: "We were at the Ambassador West. We were getting numbers and analyzing them. It didn't look good. Our supporters were in the ballroom and the mayor sent me out to tell them we were not conceding yet. I said we'd be in touch with them tomorrow. And then everyone went home. I remember walking over to a bar on Division Street. I sat at the bar and they had one of those

---

1   Steve Brown, interview.

early big screen television sets on and I watched Harold Washington and Jesse Jackson singing and dancing. I sat there alone at the bar and started to cry.

"The next day we held a news conference at the hotel. Sawyer and his assistant, Dana Herring, and I helped her prepare a statement. She gave the statement and took no questions from the reporters. We went back to the campaign headquarters and she cried. I had never seen her cry before. (Byrne in her own biography *My Chicago* had described the moment as like a death in the family.) Then Sawyer cried."[2]

Around midnight at the Hyatt Hotel, Rich Daley gave a very classy speech to about three thousand followers. As the crowd shouted, "No, no," Daley said his campaign had fallen short, but he described it as one of the brightest chapters in Chicago politics. He congratulated Washington. Daley and his family would spend the night at the hotel and then go home.

On election night, Vince Tenuto, the cop and staunch Daley supporter, was at the Hyatt Hotel. "The only two people crying at that thing were Pat Daley (Daley's sister) and myself. I was body-guarding that night. When you got off the elevator I was sitting there. I'm sitting there. I'll tell you from my heart. Rich went down to make a concession speech. Rose Bonomo came out and said we were gonna lose. I got a little emotional. Then Mrs. Daley came off the elevator. And she walked by and saw I was a little disturbed. And she gave me a little hug. And she said, 'You know what? My husband would be very proud of you.' And I'll remember that 'til the day I die. She said, 'You stood by my son. I'll never forget you for that.' When she left, Pat Daley came by. And she was bawling like a baby. And the both of us had a good cry."[3]

I'm standing in the lobby of the Hyatt Hotel with a couple of other reporters who had covered the campaign when Mrs. Daley comes by. She is beaming. Within the hour, her son Rich has made a speech before hundreds of supporters conceding defeat. He has

---

2　William Griffin, interviewed by author, Chicago, IL, December 22, 2006.
3　Vince Tenuto, interview.

come in third in a three-way race for the Democratic nomination for mayor of Chicago.

But defeat is not on the face of Sis Daley. "I'm so proud of him. He ran a good campaign. Wasn't his speech nice? Didn't you think so?"

High up in the hotel, the Daley boys have a suite. Someone comes down and invites a few of us up. They are up there with their wives and friends, drinking beer. Pictures of Jane Byrne as she left the Ambassador West appear on a couple of television screens but no one pays any attention. For the Daleys, it's over.

Rich Daley takes it upon himself to move about the room to console others. "This really wasn't so bad," he says. "When my son died, that was the worst thing that ever happened to me. This is nothing compared to that."

Bill Daley was taking it real hard. He is the youngest of the sons. And he is becoming a big political strategist and a player. He is a competitor. It is difficult for him to find any meaning in defeat that night.

"I was terrified on election night," said Steven Flowers, the Washington volunteer in the 49th Ward. "I didn't go downtown to the Washington headquarters. I was never into the parties or the groupie stuff. I was about getting the job done and counting the numbers on election night. When I heard that Harold won, I just cried most of the night. It was like, 'Now there's a ray of hope.' There's fresh air blowing through the city and the stale, stagnant way of doing things is going to be different."[4]

At Washington Headquarters in the McCormick Inn, just south of the Loop, the celebration was going gangbusters. Several thousand people had gathered and more were coming as the news spread. Traffic was becoming snarled on Lake Shore Drive. A woman in the crowd said prophetically, "Now we can go for president." It was past midnight and the crowd was excited. A master of ceremonies asked them to be patient and reminded them that there was another election to go in April. Rev. Jesse Jackson dominated the stage most of the evening of waiting. "We want it all," he proclaimed to the crowd.

---

4   Steven Flowers, interviewed by author, Chicago, IL, August 22, 2010.

Harold Washington was still in his private suite. Jane Byrne had gone home for the night without conceding defeat. Harold would not appear before his happy supporters until about 2 AM. He looked exhausted. His voice was hoarse and he had trouble talking because the crowd was wild with joy. He said he proudly accepted the Democratic nomination for mayor of Chicago. He had praise for the "graciousness" of Richard M. Daley and said Daley had pledged to support his campaign. Rev. Jackson seemed to edge his way into the center of the camera view finder. But, now, this night it was all about Harold.

Washington had won by thirty-six thousand votes out of nearly 1.3 million cast. Harold got 36% of the vote, Byrne 34% and Daley 30%. A heavy turnout in the African American wards and the division of the white vote were seen as the main ingredients for Washington's stunning victory.

Jelly Holt, the old captain from the 3rd Ward who stuck with the party organization, carried his precinct for Jane Byrne.

Big Ed Quigley, the last of the white plantation bosses on the black West Side, lost his 27th Ward big time. Washington defeated Byrne there by better than three-to-one. Big Ed probably never saw those blue Washington buttons worn by his workers during the big rally for Mayor Byrne right before the election.

Mayor Byrne also gave her support to Washington when she held her news conference the next day. She appeared as cool as she had throughout the campaign. "Once the people tell you what they want, you accept it." She left then for a vacation in Palm Springs. When someone asked her if she planned to run again for elected office, she said, "I see myself swimming this afternoon." Byrne had been asked what was left of her ten million dollar campaign fund. Although she consistently denied that she ever raised that much money, she said she hadn't looked lately and didn't know what was left. Years later, Steve McMullen, Jay McMullen's son, would say that all the money was gone after the campaign and that someone had given his father and Jane their tickets to Palm Springs.

"So I told Uncle Chester—Don't worry, Harold Washington doesn't want to marry your sister. That may seem like a strange thing to say about the next mayor of Chicago. I never had to tell Uncle Chester that Mayor Daley or Mayor Bilandic wouldn't marry his sister. On the other hand no other mayor, in the long and wild eyed history of Chicago has had one attribute of Washington. He's black." So wrote *Chicago Sun Times* columnist Mike Royko right after Washington's primary victory.

Suddenly the Epton campaign was alive. As Bernie himself had predicted, the three-way, nasty Democratic primary had left many unhappy people in the camps of the two losers. Where would they go? Where would the committeemen go? Harold had been bashing the Democratic Machine. And then there was the racial thing. Was Chicago ready to elect its first black mayor? All of this was up in the air on the morning of February 23, 1983.

Bernie Epton had many new friends and supporters on that morning. The man who had been Mr. Nobody at a big GOP dinner a couple of months earlier was now Mr. Somebody, a viable candidate for mayor of the city of Chicago.

One of those offering support was the popular Republican governor of Illinois, James R. Thompson. Thompson had just won a narrow third term victory over Senator Adlai Stevenson. During a contentious battle over a possible recount, the Thompson campaign office on Michigan Avenue remained open. During late November and December, Epton's daughter Dale was given an office there. That was the extent of the Epton campaign in those early days: daughter Dale manning the office and Bernie out making appearances before small civic groups. He was ignored by the media.

But after the primary election, Thompson's people merged into the Epton campaign. Some of the old time city Republicans, who were with Epton in the beginning, were being big-footed out of the way by the younger, more aggressive Thompson crowd.

It was a time when the Lee Atwater school of politics was in vogue in America. The feisty bantam rooster from South Carolina had shown staid, country club Republicans they could fight just as mean and nasty as the Democrats. Politics was about scheming and conniving. The object was winning above all else. The media was there to be manipulated. Sublime, half truthful messages were OK.

Thompson's camp was not short of people who could follow this playbook. James Fletcher, a former Deputy Governor and Thompson confidant, was named manager of the newly rated Epton campaign. Bernie Epton, the old time Republican, the World War II veteran, may have been overwhelmed.

But the election wasn't quite over for Mayor Jane Byrne. After a short vacation in Palm Springs, she returned to Chicago. About 150 diehard fans and pipers from the Emerald Society Band were there to greet her. The crowd shouted, "We want Jane! Write in Jane! Four more years!" The mayor was asked about the possibility of a write-in campaign, but she said she didn't think it would work.

Nevertheless, on March 16, Mayor Byrne announced she would mount a write-in campaign for mayor and spend a million dollars on advertising. But it was hard to get rid of the loser label, and her write-in effort lasted only a week. First of all, the money apparently was all gone. Her two top managers, Bill Griffin and Steve Brown, declined to participate. As Brown recalled many years later, "There was this whole situation with the write-in. And Griffin and I wanted to get far away from it. So Griffin and I went to Florida for a few days, just on the lam. We were getting calls to come back and get involved. I came back and went to Springfield to work on the city's legislative agenda."[5]

David Sawyer, the New York media advisor, stayed briefly but then learned the National Democratic Party was threatening to take his firm off their list of preferred consultants. Sawyer got the message and bowed out. So did two executives of the Merchandise Mart, Thomas King and James Bidwell, whom Byrne had enlisted for the write-in. At the time, the Merchandise Mart was owned by the Kennedy family. Senator Edward Kennedy, who had endorsed Byrne in the primary, was now campaigning for Congressman Washington. He apparently sent a message to King and Bidwell.

Byrne had asked the Board of Elections for a change in rules to make it easier for someone to write in a candidate in the election. The Board of Elections refused and her campaign was faced with a

---

5 Steve Brown, interview.

legal battle. So Byrne said thanks to all her supporters and got out. She urged everyone to vote on April 12, but she did not endorse anyone.

Still, it wasn't quite over for Byrne. A story came out of Washington, D.C., from unnamed Republican sources. It said that Jane Byrne or her representatives had approached White House political aides with a proposal to have Byrne replace Bernie Epton as the Republican candidate for mayor of Chicago. Apparently there were polls that showed Byrne had a better chance of winning.

Whether the idea got as far as President Ronald Reagan is not known. But there were reports a White House political operative had suggested Epton might agree to step down if offered some government legal business. And some of the young Turks of the Party were very interested in winning the mayor's office in a major American city like Chicago.

The White House and the Republican National Committee denied the story. So did Mayor Jane Byrne and so did Bernie Epton. But the scenario had credibility. It appeared in the *Chicago Tribune* under the byline of Jon Margolis, a highly respected Washington political correspondent with excellent sources.

Sponsors of the idea had misjudged Bernie Epton. Bernie Epton was a wealthy man. Later on, the Epton for Mayor campaign would issue a press release stating the candidate had paid $786,000 in federal income taxes and $79,000 in state income taxes over the past two years. His charitable contributions were just over $136,000. Governor James Thompson, who had endorsed Epton, was opposed to the idea.

The Margolis story quoted Republican polling sources as saying Epton could come close to beating Washington but couldn't win. It was reported that Governor James Thompson put a brick on the proposal because of the brazen racial aspect of the scheme. And certainly Epton, a lawyer worth millions, wasn't going to be bought off by some Washington legal business. Epton dismissed the whole story as just rumors.

About this same time, Wallace Johnson, a prominent businessman and Epton campaign fund raiser, told reporters an interesting story. Johnson had been the Republican candidate for mayor four years earlier when Jane Byrne had stunned the Democratic Party and defeated incumbent Michael Bilandic. Johnson said that after the primary, he was approached by top Democrats who wanted him to vacate the ticket in favor of a Machine candidate. Johnson declined and suffered the perfunctory GOP defeat in the general election.

Jim Stricklin, the talented NBC cameraman who witnessed much of the campaign.

Bill Griffin resigned from the Byrne administration and later managed her campaign.

Russ Ewing, a jazz pianist who once worked for Bob Hope, broadcast Epton's medical records.

Lindsley "Jelly" Holt carried his South side precinct for Jane Byrne. *(Courtesy WMAQ-TV NBC 5 Chicago)*

Steve Brown was the spokesperson
for the Byrne reelection bid.

James "Skinny" Sheahan worked
South side precincts for Daley.

Vincent Tenuto, a former cop who
was a driver for Daley.

Tom Manion managed North side
wards for Daley.

Steven Flowers was arrested while
putting up Washington signs on the
far North side.

Tom Carey, campaign worker and numbers cruncher for Daley.

David Axelrod, the young Tribune reporter who would later help elect the first African American President.

Renault Robinson, an activist former policeman who managed Harold Washington's campaign.

Phil Krone, a crafty political operative who advised Daley.

PART IV

The Second Election

✳ CHAPTER 10 ✳

That Racial Thing

I THINK IT WAS IN THE 35TH WARD, *a Polish neighborhood on the Northwest Side. The banquet room of a restaurant not far from the Kennedy Expressway. The all white crowd was enthusiastic, shouting, "Ber-nie, Ber-nie, Ber-nie." Suddenly, the Republican candidate for mayor of Chicago, Bernie Epton, appears. He has an entourage now. He is delighted by the reception. "Ber-nie, Ber-nie!" I remember thinking at the time, "Does he really believe this? Are they really shouting for him? Do they even know him or what he stands for? Have any of them ever seen a Republican before? Or are they really shouting, 'White guy, white guy, white guy!'"*

But that's the way it was in Chicago in those days. Everything was about race. If you walked in a tavern on the Northwest or Southwest Sides, the conversation turned to: What are we going to do about the shines? They're running a shine for mayor. In the black neighborhoods it was: What's whitey up to this time?

And I could tell you a couple of other stories about race in Chicago. One terrible incident in Marquette Park.

A black minister was leading a protest march down Western Avenue, which was then the boundary between the black and white neighborhoods. My camera crew and I parked on a side street a couple of blocks from the demonstration. As we made our way toward the march, I noticed an angry crowd of whites gathering on a side street. The crowd had slowed down a car that was driving down this street. As I came closer, I could see the car was driven by a young black woman. There was another black woman in the

151

passenger seat and two small children in the back seat. They must have been on this street by mistake. The crowd surrounded the car and started rocking it. Suddenly, two uniformed Chicago policemen arrived. Both were white. They got the women and the children out of the car and escorted them inside a nearby apartment building. Within seconds, the angry mob had turned the car over and set it afire. I can still see a little boy's eyes as he looked back on this scene when the policeman was carrying him in the building. Where are these kids today? And what do they think?

And then there can be the reverse of racism in Chicago.

One fine spring day, I'm sent to the West Side to meet Nick Comito. His modest little home is on a postage stamp lot and we're sitting in the midst of a beautiful garden that Nick has created in the tiny backyard.

It has been a year since a young black man entered the yard and shot Nick. Doctors said one of the bullets that entered his head literally exploded his eyes, blinding him for life. Nick made the news because of something he said in the hospital that startled Chicagoans. He felt no anger or hate for the young man who shot him.

A year later, Nick is learning to read Braille and to walk with a cane. The garden is real to him now only through smell and hearing and touch. Nick and his wife have decided to stay in the neighborhood. They will not move. The man who shot Nick Comito is doing 100 to 200 years. Nick still prays for him.

The racial atmosphere in Chicago had been highly charged for the primary election. Now, as the general election neared, things got even worse. Channel 5 cameraman Jim Stricklin recalled, "During the campaign I never saw the city so divided. There were families who always voted Democratic who were split between Harold and Epton. Once I was nervous about Harold's safety. We were at an Eastern Orthodox Church up off the expressway going toward O'Hare. Harold was making an appearance, but the crowd was infiltrated by Epton supporters. They were very hostile, shouting names and using the 'N' word. I remember they were passing out pens and on the pen was a picture of a half a slice of watermelon with the inscription, 'Guess who's coming to City Hall'."[1]

James Fletcher, who was running the Epton campaign, hired John Deardourff to be the campaign's media advisor and to produce Epton's television commercials. Deardourff worked out of Washington, D.C., with a partner named Douglas Bailey. But they usually worked separately on campaigns and Bailey was not involved in the Washington-Epton battle. Bailey-Deardourff and Associates had a blue chip client list of moderate Republicans that included Jim Thompson of Illinois, Nelson Rockefeller of New York, Senator Charles Percy of Illinois, New York Mayor John Lindsay and former Missouri Senator John Danforth. Bailey and Deardourff, along with some others, were considered founding fathers of the political consulting trade.

Deardourff's research showed that Chicagoans did not know much about Harold Washington's history, especially his carelessness in personal financial affairs. He determined that Epton needed to raise these issues: the failure to file income tax returns, the suspension of the law license, the building code violations and neglect of bills. Even though these issues had been raised before, they did not play a major role in the primary election. Deardourff and Fletcher reasoned that Washington's record on these personal fiscal matters was fair game in an election whose main focus was the city's precarious fiscal condition.

So along came the famous television commercial attacking Washington's personal history and ending with the tag line, "Epton, before it's too late." Epton's daughter, Dale, who was working on the campaign, questioned Deardourff about it. "Epton, before it's too late" had a chilling tone to it. It was like a time bomb about to go off, a racially charged time bomb. That's how most folks saw it after the commercial hit the airwaves.

Robert Newtson, the deputy campaign manager, blamed Fletcher for the "Epton, before it's too late" thing. "Fletcher wasn't there because he was Bernie's friend," Newtson said. "Fletcher and others were interested in electing a Republican mayor because of the rewards it would bring. In all of these campaigns there are outsiders

---

1   Jim Stricklin, interview.

who come in with these commercials and they throw a bomb and leave others to live with the mess. I think this is what happened to Bernie. Bernie does have to bear responsibility for his ads. But he was never in his heart a racist."[2] Bernie Epton argued that the line was aimed at calling attention to the city's financial crisis and the possibility of having a mayor who couldn't even manage his own finances.

Chicago Sun Times columnist Mike Royko wrote a scathing column on Bailey-Deardourff and the "Epton, before it's too late" theme. Royko recalled that the firm had been called in to handle media for a GOP candidate for governor of Virginia who was running against Charles Robb, a Democrat and son-in-law of President Lyndon Johnson. Bailey-Deardourff made commercials noting that Robb had voted in favor of an official holiday to observe Dr. Martin Luther King's birthday, an obvious appeal to the racist vote, according to Royko. Bailey-Deardourff also disclosed that Robb had voted against harsh prison terms for possession of small amounts of marijuana. "What has Robb been smoking?" the commercial asked. Said Royko, "This risk, of course, for outfits like Bailey-Deardourff is that if they get into a losing streak—Robb won—their services won't be in great demand. If that happens they'll have to drop politics and start doing commercials for other products such as toilet paper. That shift shouldn't be difficult. They'll still be in their own element."

A WOMAN IN A FUR COAT said she was ashamed of all the nasty shouting. To make a statement, she asked some of Harold Washington's entourage for a Harold button and she pinned it on her coat. One hundred fifty to two hundred demonstrators had gathered outside St. Pascal's Church to greet the black man who was a candidate for mayor. The crowd was angry and hostile. And there was hatred on many faces. Another woman burst into tears and said she was so upset she couldn't go into church. So said the *Chicago Tribune* account of what happened.

---

2   Robert Newtson, interviewed by author via phone, October 31, 2008.

St. Pascal's Catholic Church in the Portage Park neighborhood on Chicago's far Northwest Side was founded in 1914. It's an old time Chicago parish that has been the spiritual home for Polish Americans who have lived in the neighborhood for so many years. Today there's a Polish mass on Sundays and the parish recently resumed Bingo games.

In the campaign for mayor of Chicago in 1983, St. Pascal's would have its moment of fame or infamy. The incident occurred there on Palm Sunday and would have serious consequences on the election for mayor of Chicago.

On that Sunday, former Vice President Walter Mondale came to Chicago to campaign for Congressman Harold Washington. It was an important visit for Mondale. He was trying to make amends with Washington, who was the favorite to become mayor of the nation's second largest city. Mondale had made a mistake and backed Richard M. Daley in the primary election. He wanted to be the Democratic Party candidate for president against Ronald Reagan in 1984.

There are many conflicting reports about what exactly happened that day. Most of the demonstrators had Epton signs. Rev. Francis Ciezadlo had invited Washington and Mondale to his church. He said only a couple of dozen of the demonstrators appeared to be members of the parish. The rest had come from somewhere else. What went out on television that day and around the world were those angry contorted faces in the crowd.

Some of the protesters were calling Washington and Mondale baby killers, a reference to their stand on abortion rights. But Father Ciezadlo informed them that Epton was also pro-choice. Washington and Mondale entered the church but decided to leave immediately because of the disturbance taking place outside.

A disheartened Father Ciezadlo told reporters, "I hate to say we are prejudiced, but it may be so." Joseph Cardinal Bernardin, the Catholic Archbishop of Chicago, said he was saddened by the reception accorded to Mondale and Washington.

But there was more to the story. Both Washington and Epton had been invited some time earlier to a parish discussion group in the evening. Epton was unable to attend, so the event was canceled.

Father Ciezadlo and his parish council thought it would be informative for parishioners to hear the mayoral candidates on local issues, such as what would be built on a vacant city lot in the neighborhood. Later, when the Washington campaign was looking for places for Washington and Mondale to go on Palm Sunday, someone remembered the earlier invitation from St. Pascal's. Father Ciezadlo was nervous about the situation. He even consulted with Cardinal Bernardin, who had come to the church the night before to confer the sacrament of Confirmation. Bernardin advised that the invitation could not be withdrawn. The pastor informed the campaign the two men were welcome to attend mass but there would be no special seating, there should be no politicking and the media was not invited inside the church. Washington and Mondale arrived late, when mass was almost over.

A year after the election, a small book of essays on the campaign was edited by two college professors who specialized in local politics, Melvin G. Holli of the University of Illinois Chicago and Paul M. Green of Governors State University. One of the essays was written by Doris Graber, also a political science professor who was an expert on media and politics. Ms. Graber was critical of how the media covered the campaign, charging that news people alone decide "who to cover and who to ignore." She said that the incident at St. Pascal's was a good example of how the news media magnifies and misuses racial angles and racist charges. Specifically, Ms. Graber pointed out that no racial epithets came from the crowd, as was widely reported at the time, and that the booing episode differed little from incidents encountered by Jane Byrne, Richard Daley and Bernard Epton on other occasions. Yet the episode was described as a racial insult.

In the same book, two chapters later, political consultant Don Rose wrote that there were indeed racial slurs shouted against Washington and Mondale, and he took note of subsequent headlines: "Chicago's ugly election" by *Newsweek* and "Hatred Walks the Streets" by *People* Magazine.

Within a few days, Washington's media consultant, Bill Zimmerman, had gathered the video from St. Pascal's and produced some powerful television commercials. One of them intercut the screaming crowd with school children reciting the Pledge of Allegiance. Another tied the footage to scenes of the Kennedy and King assassinations.

The Washington campaign withdrew the spots from Channel 2 after CBS threatened legal action because some of their news footage had been used without permission. Channel 5 (NBC) claimed the same thing, but continued to run the commercials.

On April 6, John Deardourff and Jim Fletcher held a news conference to unveil some new Epton commercials which were much more positive than earlier spots, which attacked Washington's personal integrity. Standard operating procedure for political consultants is to go positive at the end of a campaign. There was a surprise visitor imbedded with the reporters at this news conference. It was Bill Zimmerman, Washington's media consultant. Zimmerman accused Deardourff of running the most racist campaign since George Wallace ran for president. Deardourff accused the Washington camp of racism referring to the St. Pascal's incident and the subsequent commercials. The exchange made the evening newscasts.

The accusations of racism against Epton and the St. Pascal's television commercials had a powerful impact in the waning days of the campaign. Polls showed that the election hinged on an undecided vote of about 12%. It was believed this vote was on the lakefront, the so-called lakefront liberals. They had raised an eyebrow in 1977 because of Harold Washington's legal problems. Would all of the racial stuff change their minds this time?

✳ CHAPTER 11 ✳

Opposition Research the Medical Files

IN LATE MARCH, Channel 7 reporter Russ Ewing received a phone call from a man who worked at Michael Reese Hospital on the South Side. The man told Ewing that Bernie Epton had been admitted to the psychiatric unit in the past and said he was "as nutty as a fruitcake." He gave Ewing the name of another man who worked in that area who was willing to talk about it.

"I arranged to meet with this man," Ewing said, "in the parking lot of Soldier Field. We talked for a long time. He told me the psychiatric unit was the building closest to 31st Street, off from the main hospital, and that Epton had been there. I asked him how I could confirm that and he gave me the name of a man who worked in the computer section of the hospital. He said the guy could give me a computer printout of Bernie Epton's medical records. I said that would be like gold if I could get that."[1]

Ewing never saw the man from the computer section, but an envelope was dropped off at Channel 7 with Epton's medical records. At some point during his investigation, Ewing met with Harold Washington at a church at 56th and Wabash. "I thought I would tell him about the story I was about to break on Bernie. As I approached him inside the church, he motioned me over toward a wall. He told me to face the wall when I spoke to him 'cause Epton's people had lip readers who were following him around. When I told him about the information he asked me to hold the story until

---

1 Russ Ewing, interview.

two or three days before the election because the voters have short memories. But I couldn't do that."[2]

When Ewing had secured Epton's medical records, he went to Saul Epton, Bernie's brother, who was a Cook County judge. "I showed him what I had and he immediately picked up the phone and called Bernie. He said, 'They know you've been in the hospital, you might as well talk about it.' So I went and did an interview with Bernie."[3]

The Ewing story made national news. Epton disclosed that he had entered Michael Reese Hospital's Singer Pavilion on two occasions to find out whether severe stomach and migraine headache pain he had been suffering for fifteen to twenty years was real or psychosomatic. He was later found to have stomach ulcers. He also said he had seen a psychiatrist several times between 1968 and 1975 because of arguments with his family over the Vietnam War.

"There was one bad part of the story," Ewing said. "There was a black woman who worked in the psychiatric unit who would have known Epton was there, and they blamed the leak on her. They fired this woman, but she had nothing to do with it. The guys who gave me the information were white guys. I later helped the woman get another job."[4]

Ken Bode was a national correspondent for NBC News who was sent to cover the 1983 campaign for mayor in Chicago. Bode was a veteran newsman who had been politics editor for the *National Review*. His assignment was to stay in Chicago for the duration of the campaign. He set up shop in the Water Tower Hyatt Hotel on the near North Side overlooking the historic water tower, a landmark that had survived the great Chicago Fire.

One Sunday evening, as he returned to Chicago from New York, Bode noticed the message light blinking on his phone. When he called the front desk, he was told a package had been left for him.

---

2   Russ Ewing, interview.
3   Ibid.
4   Ibid.

It was a plain, unmarked business envelope, with only his name on it. Inside was a thick packet of papers, including an admission document to the Michael Reese Hospital psychiatric unit signed by the patient himself, Bernard E. Epton. The documents included many difficult to read, handwritten doctors' notes. But it became clear that Epton had been a patient in the unit on at least two occasions, in 1975 and 1978. He had been treated for chronic headaches and stomach pain. His psychiatric diagnosis was depressive neurosis. Powerful medicines including Percodan and Demerol had been prescribed. Doctors said his condition improved at the time of discharge but they recommended continued psychotherapy twice a week.

Ken Bode decided to convene a small group of professionals from psychology and psychiatry at breakfast the next morning. Bode wanted to know if the documents were authentic and if the information was serious enough to inform the voters of Chicago before the election. The group answered yes to both questions.

The bosses at the NBC *Nightly News* Program in New York were skeptical when Bode contacted them. They wanted to know if he had stolen the papers, which he assured them he had not. Bode suggested that he work on the story with the local NBC people in Chicago. During the campaign, he had collaborated with Carol Marin, a first rate anchor/ reporter for Channel 5 in Chicago, and her equally talented producer, Don Moseley.

Bode turned the records over to Marin and Moseley, who did their own analysis of the documents with their own experts.

There was some soul searching about whether or not to run such a delicate story so close to the election. Marin and Moseley said the final decision rested on an earlier interview Epton had with Channel 5 reporter Dick Kay on the program *City Desk*. Epton had proclaimed himself to be in good health and denied having any serious issues in the past.

So, on March 30, the story of Epton and his medical records ran on the ten o'clock news on Channel 5. Epton agreed to be interviewed for the report. He denied having chronic depression. He did say that, after going to three hospitals, including the Mayo

Clinic for headaches and abdominal pain, and being told there was nothing physically wrong, he felt pretty depressed. Epton said his pain and depression in no way impaired his ability to run his law practice or be an effective legislator.[5]

The story got considerable play in the press during the last two weeks of the campaign, Epton continuing to proclaim his health was fine now. Dr. Walter Feldman, a psychiatrist and an attorney, was quoted in the *Tribune* saying, "Depression is a normal reaction to a severe illness. There's no big deal here." Epton's press secretary promised to release the candidate's entire medical records, but that never happened. When asked about his own health, Harold Washington responded, "Everything works and nothing hurts." But the media never pushed him on the issue.

Many years later, Ken Bode became a journalism professor. The Epton medical records were often a popular topic for discussion among students. The question was always, "What would you do?"

About ten days before the election, Epton issued a statement saying the taking of his medical records and their publication violated state law and he indicated legal remedies may be sought at the appropriate time.

Robert Newtson, a longtime Republican staffer in the state legislature who had a close relationship with Epton, served as deputy campaign manager for the Epton campaign. Years later, he had some thoughts about the publication of Epton's medical records: "It was kind of an open secret that Bernie, for years, had suffered from depression. But the way the story came out, it made him look like some suicidal lunatic. That wasn't the case at all. I think that, with the passage of time, looking back, his medical condition wasn't all that unusual and certainly wouldn't disqualify him from holding political office. But, at the time, and with the Eagleton incident, it was important."[6] Sen. Thomas Eagleton of Missouri was dropped as a vice presidential candidate with George McGovern in 1972 after it was revealed that he had received psychiatric treatment.

---

5   *NBC 5 News,* March 30, 1983.
6   Robert Newtson, interview.

After much wrangling between their respective handlers and advisors, Congressman Harold Washington and Bernard Epton appeared at a debate on March 21. It was a familiar setting, the auditorium of the First National Bank of Chicago. It was sponsored by the *Sun Times* and James Hoge was the moderator. This time, the dean of City Hall reporters, Harry Golden, Jr., was on the panel of questioners. He was flanked by Denise Jimenez of WMAQ radio and Clarence Page of WBBM-TV. The event received widespread television and radio coverage. It was the only debate the two men would have.

So the two combatants stood face to face to duke it out. Both men were over sixty years of age and had battled long in the halls of Chicago and Illinois politics. Years later, supporters of each man would scratch their heads and wonder why they did it. After a long career, Harold now had a safe seat in Congress. The pay and benefits were great. He could become an elder statesman. Bernie was a millionaire. He had a distinguished legislative career. He could have gone back to his prosperous law firm or do almost anything he wanted. What made him think a Republican could be elected mayor of Chicago?

Yet here they were, toe to toe, on live television. At least Harold was carrying the torch for the African American community. But why was Bernie there?

Epton had let it be known that he was going to drop a bombshell. So, in his opening remarks, Washington addressed his old "misdemeanor" tax problems and suspension of his law license. "They were over a decade old," said Washington, "and being used by Epton to obscure the issues." He charged that Epton's voting record in the General Assembly was an exact replica of President Reagan's programs.

Then came Epton's turn. He held up a black loose leaf binder which he said contained new information about the congressman. Though not a great speaker, Epton was eloquent as he made his case. He said the voters had a right to know basic things about the two candidates. "The only way I know how to judge what a person will do in the future is to know what he has done in the past. Will he obey the law? Will he tell the truth?" And he referenced the old charges, but brought up a new transgression. The black book would reveal that Washington told the state agency that reinstated his law license he had not been a party to any lawsuits. Epton charged there had been several pending in the Circuit Court of Cook County that involved failure to pay rent and numerous building code violations on a slum apartment building Harold owned with some relatives on the South Side. "Will he tell the truth?"

Harold Washington was furious. He couldn't wait to respond. "Mr. Epton said he was going to take the gloves off. What he did was take off his shoes and we found he didn't wash his feet and he didn't wash his socks." Washington admitted that he had done wrong and had been punished adequately and that he had had an exemplary record ever since. Later in the program, Denise Jimenez would ask Washington how he could just forget to file his income taxes. Washington's birthday was April 15. Harold stuck to his story. He just forgot.

There were humorous moments as the two legislators danced around each other. Epton was asked about a poll which Jane Byrne had taken. (Byrne, at the time, had announced a write-in campaign.) It showed Harold with 46% of the vote, Byrne with 33% and Epton with 16%. Epton: "Well first she arrived at the figures and then she took the poll." Much laughter from the audience and then a long pause. Finally, moderator Hoge stammered, "Is that the end of your answer, Mr. Epton?" Epton: "I think that's sufficient." More laughter. Harold: "Mr. Epton may not lead you but he'll sure tickle you to death."

✳ CHAPTER 12 ✳

The Election

I
T WAS A STRANGE CAMPAIGN. If it was strictly a racial thing, as the media and many others believed, maybe it's because the two candidates agreed on almost all the major issues. Both favored an increase in the state income tax to keep the city's schools and transportation system afloat. On abortion, both men were pro-choice, and both favored the equal rights amendment for women. On patronage, they parted ways. Washington repeatedly attacked the system, while Epton was careful to say that city patronage workers who did their jobs had nothing to fear from him. Epton hinted that maybe the appointment of a black police superintendant might be a good way to heal wounds in the city's black community.

Epton had not been well known outside of legislative circles. Most Chicagoans were wondering: who is this guy? Phil O'Connor was head of the Illinois Department of Insurance during the administration of Governor James Thompson. Even though Epton's law firm represented insurance companies, O'Connor said Epton never called the department to ask for anything. "He never asked for any favors for clients, nothing like that. We would always go to him to sponsor the more complex legislation. We would also go to him with bills that the insurance industry might not like and he would take them."[1] O'Connor described himself as kind of a shirttail advisor to Epton. Still, the Washington campaign accused Epton's law

---

1   Phil O'Connor, interviewed by author via phone, September 3, 2008.

firm of getting millions in legal fees from the insurance industry while Bernie was chairman of the insurance committee.

"I remember a defining moment early in the campaign," O'Connor said. "It was a Saturday evening and I turned on the news on television and here was Bernie out campaigning in the Lithuanian neighborhood out around 71st and Western and he was getting mobbed by the crowds. People were coming out of their houses and crowding around him as he walked down the street. And I called Jim Fletcher, the campaign manager, and I'm almost crying because, as a pro in the business, I told him, 'It's happening! It's happening!' Up until that moment the thing hadn't crystallized. Epton hadn't been recognized as a serious alternative. Until then, the media had been stomping on him. People were trying to get him off the ballot. And Bernie simply held fast. He wasn't going to throw away his opportunity because other people didn't think he was up to it. From that moment on it was a rush to the finish line. From then on it was an incredible campaign."[2]

The strangeness of the campaign was also manifest in the annual St. Patrick's Day Parade. Long a showcase for Democratic politicians, Chicagoans of Irish descent and otherwise delighted in seeing who was marching in the front row "wid dah mayor." A position in that front row told how a political career was going, who was in, who was out and who was up-and-coming.

Chicago's St. Patrick's Day Parade has always been run by Local 130 of the Plumbers Union, Democrats all. It's been that way ever since the late Mayor Daley brought the parade downtown in 1956. The plumbers run the whole show. They admit the marching units and assign their positions in the parade. They conduct the contest that selects the Irish parade queen. They select who will be the grand marshal and guest of honor of the parade. It could be a labor leader or a businessman or a bishop. The guest of honor might be a movie star who happens to be in town or a commandant of the Marine Corps. All of these selections are jealously guarded by the union, but the mayor is usually consulted each year.

---

2   Phil O'Connor, interviewed by author via phone, September 3, 2008.

The St. Patrick's Day Parade in 1983 was different. Jane Byrne was still the mayor and so, by tradition, she marched in the front row. She also had just announced her write-in candidacy. She was joined by Bill Lee, head of the Chicago Federation of Labor, and Ed Brabec of the Plumbers Union, along with her husband Jay McMullen and daughter Kathy.

A couple of hundred yards behind was George Dunne and his 42nd Ward organization. They had welcomed the party's nominee for mayor, Congressman Harold Washington, decked out in green garb with a McWashington pin on his lapel.

The Republican candidate for mayor, Bernie Epton, had his own marching unit, but it was quite a distance from the front, Unit 39A to be exact. Parade officials ordered an Epton car out of the line. It had a "Vote for Epton" sign on it and that's against the rules. A "Write in Jane Byrne" banner escaped their attention. A close friend of Epton said that Bernie, who suffered from severe headaches, had not had one during the campaign, that he loved a fight and the campaign made the headaches go away.

Each campaign had its own problems and peculiarities. Lillian Williams of the *Chicago Sun Times* wrote of two campaigns for Washington. One was headquartered downtown and run by civil rights leader Al Raby. Then there was a group called the task force that was working out in the neighborhoods, getting black folks out to vote from the housing projects. This was something the black precinct captains of the regular organization had never seen before. But the main campaign organization, Williams wrote, was still disorganized, and the candidate's schedule changed too frequently. It was the task force that seemed to be getting the real work done in the precincts.

And the Washington campaign had to deal with Rev. Jesse Jackson. The problem was keeping him out of the way. Jackson had dominated the stage and the TV cameras the night of the primary election while Washington waited to make his victory declaration. While still a great leader of the black community, Jackson was disliked by many whites. Jewish voters were especially sensitive since Jackson had befriended Palestinian leader Yasser Arafat.

Epton had his own problems. There was tension between the Thompson Republicans, who were running the campaign, and the local GOP. And then there was trouble with the candidate's chief policy advisor, Haskel Levi of the University of Chicago. Levi had been upset by the "Epton, before it's too late" slogan. Years later, he would tell Public Radio that Bernie convinced him to stay on, that once elected he would get rid of all the bad stuff in the campaign and they would do good things for the city. Then came a controversial article by William Safire in the *New York Times*. Safire was responding to a statement by Washington media advisor, Patrick Cadell, who called Epton's media attack a "racist appeal." Safire essentially said that it was fair game for Epton to attack Washington's record of failing to file income tax returns and failing to perform services for legal clients. "To give a black candidate a free ride on this," Safire wrote, "would go beyond condescension to outright bigotry...we should either stop praising the black community of Chicago for uniting behind the black candidate or stop complaining when white people show inclinations to do the same. Both actions are racist: praise both or condemn both."[3]

Levi came to the campaign office and found hundreds of copies of the Safire article ready for distribution. He had this interpretation of the article: "It basically claimed the following: If blacks can vote for blacks because they're blacks, whites can vote for whites because they're whites. And I looked at it and I just hit the roof and I took the whole pile and threw it in the garbage can. I mean it's a shallow, it's a stupid way of looking at the world. It's just false...when blacks get screwed because they're blacks, they're a legitimate interest group. What is the white interest group? I can understand a Pole voting for a Pole or a Czech voting for a Czech, but why would a white vote for another white? The only thing in this particular circumstance they have in common is they don't like blacks...I told Epton he had to repudiate this racist campaign, you gotta repudiate any people that are supporting you out of racist reasons, and if you don't I'm gone and if you don't I'm voting for Harold Washington.

---

3 *New York Times* News Service, March 30, 1983.

And Bernie said his argument is correct, Safire's argument is correct. And I said Bernie…and that's when he got pissed off. And he picked up my coat and jacket and briefcase, and he ostentatiously threw it out of the office. And he literally said: get the fuck out."[4]

Epton had a habit of flying off the handle at inopportune times. He was a featured speaker at a big Democratic dinner honoring Alderman Vito Marzullo, who had endorsed Epton's candidacy. Epton got up and launched a nasty attack on the news media, likening them to the media in Russia. He threatened legal action and invoked the "Fairness Doctrine." Then, the candidate and his entourage stormed out of the dinner, startling the crowd of one thousand Democrats, most of whom were supporting him.

Vito Marzullo is the face of the old Chicago Democratic Machine. It's not surprising that he endorsed Bernard Epton. In 1972 he endorsed Richard Nixon, having been infuriated by McGovern's people expelling Mayor Daley's delegation to the Democratic National Convention.

I have this memory of going into Vito Marzullo's ward for an election long since forgotten. We're in a storefront polling place taking pictures. There is a table of election judges, mostly female. Suddenly a woman jumps up and shouts excitedly, "The boss is coming, the boss is coming!" Just then, the little alderman comes in wearing a Chesterfield coat. He greets the women and sets down a box of candy. I turn to my camera crew and ask aloud why the woman called Marzullo the boss when she's wearing a Republican election judge badge. A uniformed policeman sitting nearby gives me a quiet smile like I'm a real dope. I realize immediately I must look like one. Marzullo appoints all the election judges, Democrat and Republican.

Another time we are filming Marzullo when he's holding office hours on "ward night." A precinct captain enters with an older African American woman who has a tale of woe. There's been a fire in the apartment and almost everything has been lost. Alderman Marzullo arranges to give her fifty dollars in cash. There's nothing to sign, no forms to fill out, no money owed. The precinct captain

---

4 "This American Life," *WBEZ Radio,* March 2009.

will help her get any government assistance she might be entitled to.
Independent politicians could never figure out how these Machine
hacks could get so many votes in Chicago.

Money for such things comes from the annual ward dinner-dance
like the one where Epton stormed out. On the tables that night is
a thick book with pictures of public officials and endorsed candi-
dates, and more than six hundred pages of paid advertising. The
most expensive ads are in the front of the book with gold borders.
There's a gold-bordered ad for Sunbeam Corporation that says,
"Best Wishes to Alderman Vito Marzullo and Hymie." No last name
for Hymie. But most of the ads are from local supporters of the
alderman, such as Wozniak's Casino and Moreno's Liquors on 26th
Street. There's an ad from Counselor's Row, a restaurant across
from City Hall that later will by bugged by the FBI and result in
some political corruption cases. Somebody must have beefed one
time about the use of strong arm tactics in selling ads for the ward
organizations. Every page in Marzullo's book is labeled at the top:
Voluntary Advertising. At the end of the book is an index of adver-
tisers. On the inside back cover is a full page ad for Bob Guccione,
Editor and Publisher, Penthouse *Magazine, wishing good luck to*
the alderman, the mayor and the 25th Ward.

Bernie's son, Jeff Epton, himself a candidate for City Council in
Ann Arbor, Michigan, was interviewed by WBBM Radio. He said
his father was a good and upright man but that he, Jeff, was closer
to Harold on the issues. When asked who he would vote for, he said
he probably wouldn't make up his mind until he got in the booth.
An irate Bernie heard the interview, called Jeff and told him he had
upset his mother. "Don't ever come home again," he told his son.

Bernie Epton did repudiate racism on several occasions during
the campaign, declaring he didn't want someone's vote if they were
voting for him because he was white. He also asked to meet with
Washington to try to find ways to deflect racism in the campaign.
But no such meetings took place.

Meanwhile, the campaign got nastier. Rumors circulated that
Harold Washington had been arrested for child molestation. No
evidence of such a charge was ever produced; still, the accusations

were dutifully reported on television. The Washington camp issued a report that Epton had exaggerated his war record.

Epton complained that the media was reluctant to report on Washington's history and then Harold fired a volley back. He accused Epton of playing with fire. "Epton doesn't know what he is doing. You cannot play with people's emotions in the form and manner he so insidiously tries to do and slink away and say, 'It's not my fault.'" When he repeated the argument later before a group of ministers, Washington added that if his supporters get the feeling that this campaign is going to turn into a race war, then it might turn bitter, evil, angry. "In that case, he warned, the campaign could get out of hand and some innocent person may wind up dead."[5]

Epton told *Tribune* reporters that Harold Washington wasn't the best candidate the black community could produce, and he said that if his ethnic group had come up with a candidate with Harold's record, he'd be ashamed. *Tribune* columnist Vernon Jarrett wrote eloquently when he countered that Epton didn't understand black history. Blacks had learned to forgive white racism years ago. They had to or they'd go crazy. He noted that the segregationist George Wallace regained the Governor's Mansion in Alabama with 40% of the black vote. African Americans were willing to forgive a man who said he had changed. According to Jarrett, Epton insulted 400,000 black Chicago voters who had forgiven Harold's mistakes years back and focused on his exemplary record since.

On April 2, the Epton campaign issued a statement saying the candidate's health was fine. Epton had a total of 34 campaign offices around the city. Twenty were operated by the Republican Party. Fourteen were independent offices such as Democrats for Epton and Hispanics for Epton. Eight Democratic committeemen formally endorsed Epton and threw the weight of their organizations behind the Republican. Others quietly looked the other way while some of their precinct captains worked for Epton. Many Byrne and Daley precinct captains went to work for the Epton campaign. And,

---

5   Paul Kleppner, *Chicago Divided: The Making of a Black Mayor* (DeKalb, IL: Northern Illinois University Press, 1985).

while Party Chairman Ed Vrdolyak endorsed Harold Washington, many considered the endorsement lukewarm. Many of Vrdolyak's people were working for Epton. Two weeks before the election, Vrdolyak met with Washington and warned him he might be the first Democrat to lose a race for mayor in 56 years. Vrdolyak's polling analysis showed that Epton could end up with a 30,000 vote lead if a million and a quarter voters came out. That high of a turnout was being predicted based on a huge demand for absentee ballots. Not surprisingly, Washington's people were suspicious of Vrdolyak's calculations.

The big gripe among Democratic ward bosses was that Harold never reached out to them. But that seemed to be a weak argument. Harold had gone up against the party organization and won. Traditionally the losers approach the winner with hat in hand.

The *Chicago Tribune* endorsed Harold. The circumstances of Epton's candidacy, the paper said, were extraordinary and distressing. The only reason Epton was a legitimate contender, according to the *Tribune*, was that he was white and Washington was black. It added that Washington would be a more successful mayor and would have a better chance of healing the deepening racial divisions in the city. No mention was made of Harold's income tax violations or suspension of his law license.

Chicago United, an interracial organization designed to promote racial harmony, took out a full page ad in Chicago newspapers. The message was that it was OK for voters to favor candidates of their own ethnic heritage. "It's a normal and healthy expression of political freedom."

The media, especially television, pounded home the idea that the contest was all about race. One night, Roger Mudd said on NBC, "The candidates are regarded by many Chicagoans as mediocre or obscure or both. Because Harold Washington is black and angry and Epton is white and rich, the contest is being watched as a referendum on racism." Said Mudd, "Chicago has been called the most segregated city in America." John Chancellor said that black and white Chicagoans had banded together in racial voting blocks.

At a rally in Bridgeport, the Mecca of Chicago Machine politics, a few Epton supporters wore bags over their heads labeled "Unknown Democrat." One woman said she decided against Washington when he refused to sign a joint statement with Epton promising to keep race out of the campaign. Another woman said she resented being called a racist for not supporting Washington. Referring to Washington's dependence on black voters, the woman said, "We're racist and he has cultural pride."

The author and Chicago icon Studs Terkel tried to soothe things in one TV interview. Referring to white ethnic neighborhoods, he said, "These are decent, hardworking people. They're frightened of change."

Chicago's police officers came out big for Epton, holding a large rally right before the election. The Fraternal Order of Police voted 23-to-1 to endorse him. The one vote for Harold came from the only black officer on the board. One officer typified the feelings about Washington: "He couldn't become a police officer because of his record. How could he run the whole city?"

Some of Chicago's top clergy, including Joseph Cardinal Bernardin and Rabbi Harold P. Smith, President of the Chicago Board of Rabbis, issued a statement. They urged all citizens to exercise their right to vote and urged that their votes be cast on the basis of the experience, wisdom and effectiveness of the candidates, rather than because of racial or religious factors.

In Ann Arbor, Michigan, thirty-five-year-old Jeff Epton, a Socialist Democrat, was elected to the City Council. A longtime liberal activist and Vietnam War protester, Jeff admitted to reporters he would have a tough time deciding who to vote for, his father or Harold Washington. Epton said many of his liberal friends wanted him to repudiate his father's campaign. But he absolutely denied that his father was a racist or anti-women.

A week before the election, the *Chicago Sun Times* published a poll showing Washington with 51%, Epton with 37% and 12% undecided.

The Sunday before the election, Bernie Epton took part in a parade on Harlem Avenue on the far Northwest Side of the city.

Five thousand people crowded the street, tying up traffic in either direction for at least twenty minutes. The crowd was friendly and enthusiastic. The event had been organized by a Republican, Roger McAuliffe, a police officer and the only Republican state representative from the city of Chicago. McAuliffe had plenty of help from Democratic precinct captains in the neighborhood. Epton held some babies that were handed to him from the crowd.

Earlier in the day, the candidate had appeared on David Brinkley's national TV program. He declined to go on *Meet the Press*, charging that one of the panelists, *Chicago Tribune* columnist Vernon Jarrett, was biased.

A man named D.M. Vuckovich wrote to the *Tribune's* Voice of The People column, "I fervently hope that Chicagoans will be color-blind when they cast their mayoral votes April 12. Let their choice be governed solely on the basis of the candidates' administrative and fiscal talents, buttressed by professional and personal integrity."

Bernie Neistein sits in his law office on LaSalle Street, just south of City Hall. It's April 1983, a week before the election for mayor. I go to see him because I don't have a clue as to who might win.

A casting director at 20th Century Fox could not have produced a better caricature of the old time Chicago ward boss. Neistein is burly. His bald head rests on his shoulders like a medicine ball. There is no sign of a neck. A huge, unlit cigar waggles in his mouth. He looks a little like Edward G. Robinson, only a hundred pounds heavier and tougher. And he's smart.

Bernie Neistein is a native of Chicago's West Side and, as a little boy, his father took him to political meetings at a place called Guyon's Paradise Ballroom. That's how he caught the political bug. In school, he had a natural gift for the violin. He was seventeen years old when he entered law school in 1934 and graduated number one in his class. He became a precinct captain in the 29th Ward. He was good at it, delivering the precinct 603-to-3 for Richard J. Daley in Daley's first primary election for mayor. Neistein had been a paratrooper in World War II and won a battlefield commission.

He went on to become ward committeeman and a state senator in Springfield. He stayed on as ward committeeman long after the

29th Ward went all black, maintaining an address on West Harrison Street while living at the posh Carlisle where Michigan Avenue meets Lake Shore Drive. The day I see him right before the '83 election, Bernie is sixty-six years old and retired from politics. He tells me he has a violin lesson that afternoon. Late in life, he has resumed his boyhood passion and is now playing local recitals and concerts. We reminisce a bit about his days in the legislature. "There was so much bullshit flying around down there," he says, "you had to go into the men's room for a breath of fresh air." But I'm anxious to get his opinion about the current campaign.

"Bernie, who's gonna win this thing?" I ask.

"Washington," he replies without hesitation.

"How do you figure?"

"He's gonna win."

"But Bernie," I argue, "what about the income tax and all that stuff?"

"So he didn't pay his bills. People in this town can identify with that. He's had a brush or two with the law. He's been before a grand jury. He didn't file his income tax returns. He had to do a little time. This is my kind of guy."

"You really think he's gonna win?" I persist.

Neistein: "Yeah."

It's election night, April 12, 1983. I'm covering the campaign headquarters of Bernie Epton at the Palmer House Hotel. The news is pretty good for Epton. He is in a very tight race with Democratic Congressman Harold Washington. It's been a nasty, nasty campaign. I have put in a request for an interview with the candidate who is huddled with advisors in a suite upstairs. Finally, the word comes down that Bernie will do an interview with me. For some unknown reason, Bernie Epton likes me. As I mentioned earlier, he wanted me to be his press secretary. I declined.

When I enter the Epton suite with my camera crew, I notice Governor Jim Thompson and his wife Jayne draped over a bed, watching returns on television. Sitting in front of the bed in straight chairs closer to the TV are Bernie, Lieutenant Governor George

Ryan, former state Representative Pete Peters, and former House Speaker W. Robert Blair.

In the interview, I'm taken aback by the candidate's bitterness. He attacks members of the press. "Mike Royko, Roger Simon [both Sun Times columnists] are slime," Epton says. "Vernon Jarrett [Tribune columnist] is a bigot." He says, "All the black people hate me. I represented an integrated community. Even Harold hasn't called me a racist."

I'm thinking to myself, "Why the hell is he so bitter?" The race isn't over yet. He still has a good chance of winning. That's what we all were still saying on television. But everyone in Epton's suite in the Palmer House knew the real score.

The next morning, Bernie Epton left for a Florida vacation. He said he had tried to call Harold to congratulate him but was unsuccessful. So he sent a telegram instead. He said he was sending his brother Saul to a unity breakfast the next morning.

On election night, the Washington campaign was headquartered at Donnelly Hall of McCormick Place. Ten thousand people came to witness the historic event. This time, Harold would not have to wait for the wee hours to declare victory.

Channel 5 cameraman Jim Stricklin could see it all from the photographers' platform. "The place was mobbed and everyone was going wild. I was on the camera platform for hours. When the first politicians got up to speak, I figured this would be a good chance to go to the bathroom because Harold wouldn't be far behind. I went in the men's room and there was a black guy, lying on the floor stark naked except for his socks. He was obviously dead drunk. But somebody got him and took everything but his socks. They left him his socks. So there were some roughnecks in the crowd too. But most of the people at Donnelly Hall were happy. Harold was led to the stage by state Senator Richard Newhouse and everyone was holding hands and singing, 'All this love, all this love for you,' the song by Debarge. It was an important night because the black community had never seen a victory like this before."[6]

---

6   Jim Stricklin, interview.

In his victory speech, Washington asked his supporters to rededicate their efforts to help heal the wounds that had plagued the city. "History was made tonight. I want to reach out my hand in friendship and fellowship to every living soul in this city."

Washington won by just over 48,000 votes out of nearly 1.3 million votes cast. There was a huge turnout, 82% of the registered voters. Voting was especially heavy in the black wards.

Years later, some Epton people would claim that the FBI had investigated thousands of fraudulent ballots in the election. But, if there was such an investigation, nothing ever came of it and there was nothing reported in the media. Still, some eyebrows were raised as Washington racked up 99% of the vote in nine African American wards. If there was any theft going on in this most-watched of elections, it's certain both sides were doing it, as Richard Nixon found out when he lost Illinois to John F. Kennedy in 1960. Local political folklore had it that Mayor Daley stole the election for Kennedy. Nixon decided against a recount. He knew that, if the Daley Machine had stolen votes, then the DuPage County Republican organization, headed by the cagy Elmer Hoffman, probably stole just as many. Epton may have faced a similar dilemma.

There had been reports of vote fraud during the primary election. Steve Brown said the Byrne campaign had received information that some African American wards had turned out 105% of the registered voters. Long afterward, former state Representative Phil Collins, a Republican from the suburbs, recalled running into a Democratic colleague right after the April election. It was a time when there was still camaraderie in our legislative bodies. The man's name was Marco Domico, a state representative and longtime Machine guy out of Vito Marzullo's 25th Ward. Collins said Domico had this comment on reports of over voting: "Can you believe it, Phil, we taught them how to do it and they did it."

Ray Ewell, the veteran South Side lawyer and state legislator, had this to say about voting patterns in the African American neighborhoods of Chicago: "The basic theory of the Machine was that blacks would not vote unless you paid them. And there was so-called 'walk around money' distributed in the black districts. What they had to remember is that blacks really didn't have much to vote for. The walk around money started out with the committeeman, who took a great slice of it, say maybe half of it. The other half might have gone to the precinct captains, and the captains would take their share, and very little of it would go to the people who were actually voting. And in those days, the Machine could manipulate the vote pretty good. The theory was that if you don't give the blacks any money, don't worry about it 'cause they're not going to vote. The shock was the blacks came out and voted for Harold and they got no money."[7]

To this day, the political scientists, the media, the pundits look back on the election of 1983 and say it was all about race, black versus white. One of the most reasoned analyses of the election came not from a political expert, but from a professional psychologist who had an inner city Chicago practice. Dr. Theophilus E. Green, a consultant with Associated Psychological Services, and himself an African American, wrote an op ed piece in May of 1983 in the *Chicago Tribune* that was headlined, "White racism charges overblown." Dr. Green said that Washington had some serious liabilities, which many voters were justified in choosing not to overlook. Washington's failure to provide services for legal clients was the most serious, according to Dr. Green, and those charges against his professionalism were as justified as if he were a doctor charged with amputating the wrong leg. He pointed out that Washington had threatened to dismantle the decades-old patronage system and then expected party regulars whose lives and careers depended on that system to embrace him with affection after the primary.

"For many whites in this country, their exposure to blacks is still pretty much ceremonial. They see the skycap at the airport, the cab driver in the city, the dancer on television. As a psychotherapist with a large city practice, I've found that many do not understand the culture of black people. Many of them don't have best friends who are black or daughters who want to marry outside their race. As such, the black race for many white people is foreign, alienating

---

7   Ray Ewell, interviewed by author via phone, April 30, 2008.

and threatening, filled with only the stereotypes of their imagination. The clash of cultures, the white culture and value system versus the black culture and value system is as understandable and justified as Catholic versus Protestant. The election tallies indicate that in most interracial neighborhoods where racial culture clashes were not as strong, Washington did far better than he did in those that have always been predominantly white.

"There were other white people who had a lot of good reasons not to vote for Washington, yet chose to overlook them. I don't think they did it for his color alone. His color alone would not explain his stand on the issues, his powerful executive presence and his moving oratory of concern for the common man. Washington has come into office with a different mandate than others who have held his position. He basically asked to be judged on his own terms and won a very heated campaign despite personal, political and traditional setbacks that would have stopped hundreds of others. For a black man, that has so rarely been the case.

"His election is not so much a triumph of blacks and cosmopolitan whites over traditional prejudices, but the power of an individual to be accepted on his own terms by us all. He is thus a true American original, formed by the clay of his own hands: the 'American Dream' in action. It will be interesting to see what buildings he builds, what trees he plants, what roads he paves and where they take us."[8]

---

8   Dr. Theophilius E. Green, "White Racism Charges Overblown," *Chicago Tribune,* May 3, 1983.

PART V

Epilogue

✳ CHAPTER 13 ✳

Where Are They Now?

O N APRIL 29, 1983, Harold Washington was sworn in as mayor of Chicago. He was sixty years old. The ceremony at Navy Pier included an orchestra and a children's choir. They played Aaron Copland's "Fanfare for the Common Man." Poetry was read by Gwendolyn Brooks, the Poet Laureate of Illinois, and author Studs Terkel.

In his inaugural address, Washington painted a bleak picture for the city. The financial condition was horrible. The schools faced a $200 million deficit, 100 million more than was thought during the campaign. The city was short $150 million and the transportation system was $200 million in the red. He accused Byrne of padding the city payroll with hundreds of jobs during the closing days of her administration. He said that millions would have to be cut from city expenditures and hundreds of employees would be let go. Cuts would begin in the mayor's office. He would cut his own pay by 20%.

"Business as usual will not be accepted by the people of this city. Business as usual will not be accepted by this chief executive of this great city." He promised to freeze hiring and pay raises. Unnecessary city programs would be ended. The city's financial records would be open for public view.

It was the tone of Washington's speech more than his words that frightened many of the aldermen and old ward bosses. Most had friends and relatives on the payroll. Was this all about to change?

Steve Brown, Mayor Byrne's old campaign spokesman, was still on the city payroll and went to the swearing in ceremony. "Harold made all these strident comments about the mayor and the changes he was going to make. And I remember Ed Vrdolyak nearly running people over with his car as he left the pier. And Eddie said, 'I hope he's bringing his lunch 'cause it's going to be a long battle'."[1]

Harold Washington probably could have won over many of the Democratic aldermen and committeemen after the primary election. All he had to do was reach out to them. Historically, they didn't want to make waves. All they wanted was their little piece of the pie and hold on to their little territory in the old Chicago feudal system.

But Harold had set himself up as a reformer. He had threatened the committeemen in the white wards. He was going to dance on the grave of patronage. This solidified his African American base, which delighted in watching Harold swat around these groveling white ward heelers.

Once elected, Harold was on a platform of reform and it wouldn't do to put his arms around those sleazy politicians who gave jobs and contracts to their relatives and friends. The only problem with being a reformer is that, once you're in office, it's inevitable that you too will give a job to a nephew or a niece. Or a lawyer friend suddenly becomes the attorney for a major bond issue. The thing about reformers is the way they explain this contradiction. They usually say, "Yes, I have this many relatives on the payroll and yes, my wife's Uncle Frank got that paving contract. But, don't you understand, it's OK, I'm the good guy. We're the reformers."

One of the first things the new mayor did was send word to his opponents that he was going to reorganize the City Council. Vrdolyak was to step down as chairman of the powerful zoning committee. Vrdolyak said that Washington was attacking his masculinity. He put together a majority of 29 votes on the 50-member council. Washington could only muster 21. Thus began a three-year battle between the executive and the legislative that came to be known as Council Wars. It could be nasty, like the time Washington told Vrdolyak he might get a mouthful of something he didn't want. But there were some funny moments too. One day, Vrdolyak

---

1 Steve Brown, interview.

thanked the mayor for a tip he gave him on a horse called Sweet Harold. Vrdolyak had won a couple of hundred dollars on the horse. "It would be better if you divided the profits," Washington said from the podium. "I've been trying to get you to do that for the last year," Vrdolyak replied.

At one point, Alderman Eddie Burke charged that Washington had not filed his ethics statement on time, a violation whose penalty was forfeiture of office. Eventually a judge dismissed the matter, saying that the drastic penalty had never been enforced in the state.

The "Council Wars" label came from comedian and political satirist Aaron Freeman, who wrote a hit show based on the City Hall foibles. Modeled loosely after the popular movie *Star Wars*, Freeman played all the parts, which included Harold Skytalker, Jess Jacksolo and Lord Darth Vrdolyak.

Meanwhile, Harold charmed the pants off everybody, news media and public alike. His broad smile and deep baritone voice were a winning combination. Chicagoans weren't used to a mayor who was so articulate.

He would delight audiences, like the time he talked about destroying the old Machine patronage system: "It's gone, it's gone, it's gone! And in the words of Corneal Davis, they said it wasn't dead, so I went to its grave. And I walked around that grave and I stomped on that grave and I jumped up and down and I called out, 'Patronage, Patronage, are you alive?' And Patronage didn't answer. It's dead. It's dead. It's dead. Period. And if you see Mr. Vrdolyak, tell him it's dead."

Tribune reader Ed Chensky wrote, "The 'Dese, Dem and Dose' days are gone, at least for the next four years. Harold Washington has to be the most flowery orator ever to run for the office of mayor. Now, if he can succeed in keeping the city councilmen from nodding when he addresses that august body, he may yet accomplish much that he promised during the campaign. On second thought, he may succeed even better if they do nod."

There was an old saying around the City Hall press room that you can't be around the Hall for long without getting hit by some falling corruption. Harold Washington, like mayors before him and those who came after, had an interesting episode during his first term. Clarence McClain was a South Side street guy who had worked hard for Harold's election and was given the title of advisor in the new administration. McClain had two noticeable problems. He had a big mouth, and wore one of the most outlandish hair pieces ever seen in downtown Chicago. He did a lot of bragging around town about his closeness to the mayor and that he was the guy to see if you needed something at the Hall. Pretty soon, the news media, often at the urging of Vrdolyak's people, got on Clarence McClain's case. Washington's top people were aghast when it was reported that McClain was convicted of being a pimp when he was a young man. He was eventually banned from City Hall. But the raging went on.

McClain eventually got caught up in a federal probe called Occupation Incubator, which was investigating bribes paid for city contracts. The feds planted a mole in the Lake Point Towers Apartment building, where he lavishly entertained politicians while agents next door taped everything, sometimes calling the mole on the phone and prompting him to ask certain questions. The mole was a career criminal named Michael Raymond, a con man who Florida police wanted for questioning in a couple of murder cases. Florida cops were irritated that he was getting such federal protection. The feds claimed he was on an important mission.

Eventually, McClain, four aldermen and a clerk of the circuit court went to prison. The US attorney and the FBI, who always manage to keep their shirts clean, were very quiet some years later when Michael Raymond was convicted in the murder of a bank teller who was to testify against him in another case.

Washington was not connected to this corruption. He was dusted up a little because he refused to denounce his friend Clarence McClain.

Harold Washington did the reform routine flawlessly. Before long, the African American community and a nice percentage of the "progressive whites" saw Harold as this wonderful black man trying to clean up a corrupt city and being thwarted at every turn by a bunch of nasty white obstructionists. In this sense, Harold totally outfoxed Eddie Vrdolyak.

Renault Robinson says that Vrdolyak and Mayor Washington eventually made a deal. They began talking together and had private meetings at Washington's apartment. "They kept it very personal and private and we kept it that way too." Justice Charles Freeman said that Harold enjoyed these sessions with the savvy and charming Vrdolyak. They had to meet to work out some of the routine details of running the government. But publicly, the war was still on.

After three years of Council Wars, Harold Washington caught a break. A federal court ordered special elections in some of Chicago's wards. Washington soon gained a slim majority on the City Council. He was able to make appointments and implement his programs.

It was almost time for reelection and the opponents were lining up. Washington's first term was a topsy-turvy affair. But the worst fears about Chicago having its first black mayor never materialized. City Hall was not moved to the South Side. The garbage was picked up. Police and fire services were maintained. The new mayor seemed to be a competent administrator, although some City Hall veterans wondered about the hours Washington put in. But Washington supporters countered that Harold was a night person.

So the election campaign was somewhat subdued. Jane Byrne ran again in the primary against Harold but was soundly defeated. Some of the organization wards and Daley's people had gone over to Harold. Washington also increased his support on the lakefront and among Hispanic voters. A few incidents brought back memories of the campaign four years earlier. An appellate court justice, Eugene Pincham, proclaimed that any man south of Madison Street who didn't vote for Harold ought to be hung. Some of the more outrageous acts in this election were relegated to the aldermanic races. In the 23rd Ward on the Southwest Side, a candidate named Wayne Straza obtained a photo of his opponent with Pope John Paul II. He doctored the picture by taking the Pope out and putting in Mayor Washington and Israeli Prime Minister Shimon Peres, in a blatant appeal to anti-black and anti-Jewish prejudices. Straza later apologized when he was cited by a fair election group. But it was pretty tame compared to four years earlier. The *Chicago Tribune* even called it "classy."

In the April general election, Washington faced two challengers: his old foe, Alderman Edward Vrdolyak, who ran on the Illinois Solidarity Party ticket; and a blue chip business professor recruited by the Republicans, Donald Haider. Assessor Thomas Hynes, a Daley ally, had been a candidate on the Chicago First ticket, but got weak-kneed and withdrew two days before the election. Harold won easily with 53% of the vote. But Vrdolyak showed some muscle with 41%. The Republican Party was back to square one. Its candidate, Haider, could only get 4% of the vote. But everything was looking good for Harold Washington. The losers called for unity. It appeared Washington would gain more control of the City Council. Harold gleefully proclaimed that he would be mayor for twenty years. The *Chicago Tribune* said it was looking forward to a fresh new start for the Washington administration.

But it was not to be. Harold Washington had not taken care of his health, and it began to catch up with him after his reelection. He never seemed to have time to eat a proper meal, opting instead for fast food or chocolate doughnuts. Like most World War II veterans, he struggled off and on with cigarette smoking. His friend and biographer Dempsey J. Travis tried to get the mayor to see a doctor, but the appointments were always canceled. Likewise, Travis' gifts of exercise equipment went unused. Travis recalled hearing the mayor's labored breathing during a radio show.[2]

Shortly after 11 AM on November 25, 1987, the day before Thanksgiving, the Chicago Fire Department alarm dispatcher received a call from the mayor's office. A woman's distressed voice said they needed paramedics at the mayor's office, room 507, City Hall. It was an extreme emergency. Mayor Washington's press secretary, Alton Miller, was in the office at the time. He thought the mayor was reaching to pick up a pen but then saw that the mayor had collapsed. Paramedics rushed to the office and then the mayor was taken to Northwestern Memorial Hospital, where teams of doctors worked on him for two hours before he was pronounced dead. Harold Washington was sixty-five years old.

---

2   Travis, *Harold: The People's Mayor.*

Jim Stricklin of NBC recalled an incident during the campaign. "One of Harold's favorite restaurants was a soul food place called Izola's on 75th Street. And one time when we were covering him, he stopped there to eat. Don King, the fight promoter, was in there and Harold sat with him. They brought Harold a plate of greens and ham hocks. And he started pouring salt on it. And Don King took the salt shaker away from him. I couldn't hear what they were saying exactly, but he was, like, scolding Harold. 'What are you doing with this?' I never even thought about Harold's health at that time, and I didn't even roll the camera. But I remember that scene of Don King grabbing his hand and taking the salt shaker away from him."[3]

The day that Harold Washington died I watched it all on television at home. Watched my colleagues doing the live reports from City Hall and the hospital. I had left broadcasting the year before to try to carve out a new career for myself. I was producing a play at the time. It was bittersweet to watch this major news event and not be a part of it. I had started in the business when President Kennedy was murdered. It brought back memories of Bobby Kennedy and Dr. King and the death of Mayor Richard J. Daley. Hundreds of thousands of people came to City Hall and the Daley Plaza that weekend and stood for hours in the rain, waiting to pay their respects to Mayor Washington. His body lay in state until midnight Sunday in the rotunda of City Hall. That Sunday night, I drove my son Matt downtown so he could catch a bus back to the University of Iowa, where he was a freshman. I was worried about the crowds because the bus station was on Randolph Street, across from City Hall. As we walked toward the station, Matt stopped and was somewhat overwhelmed. I realized a young man like him had never seen anything like this before. Thousands of people were in the streets, many of them in tears. He asked if we could go in and see the mayor. I told him that wasn't possible, the line was too long and he'd miss his bus. Just then, in true Chicago fashion, a man approached us. He must have recognized me from television. "Do you want to see

3   Jim Stricklin, interview.

the mayor?" he asked. I told him we didn't have time to wait. I think he was a plain clothes policeman because Matt and I were whisked in a side entrance, said a prayer by the mayor's casket and were on our way.

Harold Washington was known for fairness in his handling of city government. Services were distributed equitably to all neighborhoods. He set affirmative action goals for hiring and awarding of city contracts. And, after breaking the City Council log jam, he was just getting started. More than anything, Harold Washington, the big bear of a man with the infectious smile, was a genuine hero for Chicago's African American community.

He was an inspiration to a new generation of black Chicagoans interested in public service. He recruited Mary Flowers, a community activist on the South Side, to run for the state legislature. "Thank God he came into my life," Ms. Flowers would say years later. "He saw things in me that I never saw myself." Representative Flowers is still a member of the Illinois House.

Bernie Epton never got over the election of 1983. "He was a bitter and broken man," his brother Jerry said. "From the night of the election on, there wasn't much communication between us. And we had been very close. I didn't see him much in Florida after that."

In 1987, when Harold Washington was completing his tumultuous first term, the *New York Times* News Service speculated about a Republican candidate for mayor of Chicago, but made no mention of Epton, who had come so close to defeating Harold. Author Thomas Landess called Epton to see if he was going to run again. As caustic as ever, Epton told him, "Sure, I've just been drafted by a citizens' committee, but I probably won't be endorsed by the Republican Party." When asked if the press knew he had been drafted, Epton replied, "Of course they knew, I told them I've already been booked on a couple of talk shows."

A blue-ribbon committee of Republicans, headed by the former U.S. attorney Dan Webb, recommended Donald Haider to be the Party's candidate for mayor. Haider was a former Northwestern University business professor. Still, Epton said he would run in the primary. But the Epton campaign had not been astute in filing its petitions. The Chicago Democratic Machine has always had Draconian rules for becoming a candidate, making it easy to get rid of unwanted strangers seeking office. A disgruntled Republican from the 11th Ward, who said the Epton campaign owed him money from four years earlier, filed a challenge to Epton's petitions. It turned out the campaign had not filed enough extra signatures to offset faulty ones, and the Board of Elections Commissioners ruled that Bernard Epton was disqualified from the primary election. Bernie took it graciously and decided not to fight it. He said the Board of Elections was right in its decision. Then he disappeared from the political scene.

In December, Bernie and his wife of forty-three years, Audrey, went to visit their son Jeff and his family in Ann Arbor, Michigan. On the morning of the thirteenth, Audrey tried to awaken her husband but he was unresponsive. She called the paramedics, who tried to revive him, but he was gone. Bernie Epton was sixty-six years old. He died less than three weeks after the death his old rival, Harold Washington.

In the *Tribune* obituary, Lieutenant Governor George Ryan said Bernie had told him he had a private breakfast meeting with Mayor Washington. "Bernie said the mayor had asked that he serve on some city commission. I think it was a way the mayor could say publicly how much he respected Bernie. One of the biggest regrets Bernie had was the label of racist," Ryan said. "Nothing he ever did, either in private or public, was racist, and that label really bothered him."

The cause of Epton's death was an apparent heart attack. His son Jeff says he died of a broken heart. "My father was angry and bitter after that election, and then just sad until his life ended. I had many disputes with my father, but he was the most important figure in my life. I have more of him in me than anyone else."[4]

Jeff Epton says Harold Washington told some people privately that all the racial stuff during the campaign wasn't Bernie. He said Bernie had been his friend.

---

4   Jeff Epton, interviewed by author, Chicago, IL, January 13, 2004.

Jane Byrne wasn't through with politics after the 1983 primary election. In 1987, she lost again to Harold in the Democratic primary. In 1988, she ran unsuccessfully for clerk of the Circuit Court against Aurelia Pucinski, daughter of her onetime supporter, Alderman Roman Pucinski. She skipped the 1989 special election after Mayor Washington's death. In 1991, Byrne came in a poor third in the Democratic primary. The turnout was very low. All of the fervor and excitement of a decade earlier seemed to have faded. Even the African American candidate, Danny Davis, didn't fare very well, losing to Richard M. Daley by two-to-one.

After that, Jane Byrne faded from the scene. She appeared in a few television commercials and made an occasional speech. Her husband, advisor and onetime spokesperson, Jay McMullen, died of cancer in 1992. She published a book called *My Chicago* and she experienced a blessing not everyone gets, which may be much better than all the power and celebrity of politics. Her daughter Kathy had a son. Since then, the boy named Willy and her daughter, a successful attorney, have been the central focus of Jane Byrne's life. She has had some health issues in recent years, according to friends, but remains quite active.

The feud between Richard M. Daley and Jane Byrne never really ended. After Daley was elected mayor in 1989, Jane Byrne's name didn't appear on invitation lists for civic ceremonies. But after sixteen years in office, things thawed somewhat when Daley sent a handwritten invitation to Byrne. It was to the renewal of a Vietnam War memorial, which Byrne had originally dedicated in 1982. Byrne couldn't attend because of recent eye surgery, but her daughter and grandson represented her.[5]

Jane Byrne still lives in the Gold Coast High Rise where she lived as mayor over thirty years ago. The apartment has a splendid view of Chicago. What does she see? And does she ever have an urge to pick up the phone?

Following Harold Washington's sudden death, the City Council held a raucous meeting to select an interim mayor. After a lot of

5 *WLS-TV,* July 2006.

screaming and aldermen jumping on their desks, a reluctant Alderman Eugene Sawyer, whose nickname was "Mumbles", was elected. He was liked by most of the members. The black community was outraged because they saw him as an "Uncle Tom" type.

Richard Daley stayed away from this battle and the previous Council Wars and continued to serve as Cook County state's attorney. In 1989, a special election was held to fill the unexpired term of Harold Washington. With his strong campaign organization still in tact, Daley won easily and was reelected five more times, defeating his old enemies Byrne and Vrdolyak along the way. He broke his father's record of more than twenty-one years in the mayor's office.

Daley put together a coalition of white ethnics, African Americans, lakefront liberals and Hispanics. Everybody seemed to be happy and Daley kept getting reelected. He was a beneficiary of the economic boom of the nineties. His brother Bill was Secretary of Commerce under President Clinton. New buildings were going up in the Loop. Donald Trump came to town and built a hotel and condominium tower on the river where the Sun Times-Daily News building once stood. A fabulous Millennium Park went up on Michigan Avenue at a huge cost to the taxpayers. Neighborhoods were being rehabbed and new condominium projects were popping up everywhere. Expensive homes went up near the notorious Cabrini Green Housing project. Cabrini Green and other public housing projects were gradually being torn down.

In 1996, the Democratic National Convention came to Chicago and re-nominated President Clinton and Vice President Al Gore. It went off without a hitch. Like his father thirty years earlier, Daley encouraged the building of new fences around town to make things look nice. The son upgraded to wrought iron instead of the old stockade style.

But there were some bumps in the road. Some of Mayor Daley's closest aides were convicted of rigging city job applications to favor political allies. In 2003, Daley ordered the destruction of Meigs Field, a popular lakefront airport in downtown Chicago that handled commuter and private aviation flights and had been operating since 1948. The demolition took place in the middle of the night. Giant X's were carved where the runways were. There was no notice given to the Federal Aviation Administration, nor to owners of planes at the airport that had no place to take off. One flight had to be diverted because it had no place to land. The aviation world was stunned. But Daley got away with it and was reelected. Most recently, the city has been rocked by gang violence; often, young school children have been victims in the crossfire. Police officers in uniform have been shot in daylight. And then the economy has tanked. A major defeat for the city was its loss of the 2016 summer Olympics after a highly promoted bid that included the help of President Obama and Oprah Winfrey.

On the plus side, Daley oversaw a major expansion of O'Hare Airport and, while other rust belt cities declined, Chicago survived as a new, world class, high tech city.

Richard M. Daley's children grew up while he was in office and the mayor is now a grandfather. His wife, Maggie, has been battling cancer. In September of 2010, he surprised many in the world of politics by announcing he would not seek reelection. His polling numbers were not good. And, as he said in his announcement, "It was time for me and Chicago to move on." In 2011, Chicago got a new mayor, Rahm Emmanuel, who had been President Obama's chief of staff. In one of the great political horse trades, the Daley organization offered no opposition to Emmanuel. Daley's brother, William, took Emmanuel's place as chief of staff to the president.

Edward Vrdolyak gave up his City Council seat after losing to Washington. He turned it over to his brother, Victor, a retired high-ranking policeman. He later became a Republican and lost a race for circuit court clerk of Cook County. Although active in some Republican circles and campaigns, he never ran for public office again. He worked in his successful law practice and, for awhile, had a radio talk show with popular African American personality Ty Wansley. The brash Vrdolyak often joked about his many appearances before grand juries. Then, at age seventy, he was indicted by one, in connection with a real estate scheme. He pleaded guilty and, since no money ever changed hands, a federal judge gave him probation. Later, however, a federal appeals panel said Vrdolyak needed to do some jail time and sent it back to a new judge. At this writing, Vrdolyak was serving a short term at the federal prison in Terre Haute, Indiana.

Before leaving City Hall, Vrdolyak was interviewed by the *Tribune* and asked about leading the white majority against Harold Washington. "It was inevitable when I took on this mayor, the city's first black mayor, that someone would say I was a racist. People's first responses were visual. He was black and I was white. Unfortunately, many people never moved beyond that assessment. The thing I know I did wrong, though, was that sometimes I was too loud. Sometimes I should have lowered my voice—not softened my opposition, just the tone of it. I got angry, and when you're angry you do things that maybe you shouldn't."

Many years later, Ray Ewell, the former South Side state representative, said, "Contrary to popular thought, Vrdolyak was the furthest thing from a bigot that I've ever known. He had only one criteria and that is you're a Vrdolyak person. You're my guy. It didn't matter. He was one of the few standup people and I would say this anywhere. If you were his guy, it didn't matter if you were black, green, purple, white or any other color. That was Vrdolyak."[6]

After his defeat by Jane Byrne in 1979, Michael Bilandic went back to private law practice. Later, he was elected to the Illinois Appellate Court and then the Supreme Court in 1990, where he served as Chief Justice for two years. He died in 2002 at the age of seventy-eight.

Steve Brown, the Byrne spokesperson, was one of the first people fired when Harold Washington took over. He wasn't surprised. He had been the main spokesman for the Byrne campaign. He still had contacts in Springfield and was given a temporary job by House Speaker Michael Madigan. Later, he became Madigan's spokesperson and remains there today.

Bill Griffin, Byrne's campaign manager and the former *Tribune* reporter, went to law school. He became a successful government affairs attorney specializing in transportation issues. Today he's a public relations executive in Chicago.

---

6   Ray Ewell, interview.

James "Skinny" Sheahan, the Daley precinct organizer, helped Daley win the mayor's office finally in 1989. He was rewarded with the plum post of Director of the Mayor's Office of Special Events. Later, Daley appointed him to an executive post at McCormick Place, the city's exposition center. He retired in 2010. He's not happy with the politics of today. "It's all television commercials and consultants now, and money. It used to be people in the neighborhoods participating. We called it democracy."[7]

Don Rose, the old leader of independent politics, is still active. He wrote a popular blog supporting the presidential campaign of Barack Obama. After all these years as a reformer, he must wonder if it isn't better to lose in a good fight. When elected, some of the reformers get just as tainted as the old party hacks.

Jim Stricklin, the NBC News cameraman with the talented eye, is retired now. Not too many years ago, a young lawyer moved into his neighborhood on the South Side. His name was Barack Obama, and Stricklin watched his career take off. Today he says, "We love our president but we hope he stays in Washington a long time. When he's in town the traffic is a bitch."[8]

Russ Ewing, the versatile television reporter who broke the story about Bernie Epton's psychiatric treatment, is retired and living on a lake near Paw Paw, Michigan. He still loves his music, plays piano and has helped a neighbor child take violin lessons. Too old to fly his own plane anymore, he makes radio-controlled model airplanes and flies them around the lake.

David Axelrod decided to get out of journalism. He ventured out on his own and helped manage Paul Simon's successful campaign for the United States Senate. He did media for Richard Elrod, who was trying to retain his job as Cook County Sheriff. By the time Harold Washington was running for reelection, Axelrod had signed on as a media consultant to the campaign. He found he had a knack for creating a message and he found a talented producer who knew how to make it into a television spot.

---

7   James "Skinny" Sheahan, interview.
8   Jim Stricklin, interview.

Axelrod formed his own firm and engineered election campaigns for dozens of candidates around the country, winning 80% over a six-year period. He also became rich, by beat reporter standards. And he got close to the old Democrats of Chicago, advising Mayor Richard M. Daley, Congressman Dan Rostenkowski and Cook County Board President George Dunne.

The *Chicago Tribune* quoted one of President George W. Bush's media people as saying David Axelrod is "as good as it gets."

Then, of course, Axelrod hooked up with a young state senator named Barack Obama who would become the political phenom of the early twenty-first century. Axelrod would be one of the masterminds of the 2008 campaign that would carry Obama to the White House.

Renault Robinson, the cop who fought City Hall on behalf of minority officers and who played such a major role in Harold Washington's election, was hired as chairman of the Chicago Housing Authority by the new administration. Although his tenure was a bit bumpy, the *Chicago Tribune* praised his gracefulness in helping reform that much neglected agency. Today he runs his own temporary staffing agency in Chicago.

Tom Carey, the numbers maven, was a key factor in Daley's election as mayor in 1989. He never really was interested in any big political positions. He later dabbled in several local campaigns and still gets a twinge when the election cycles roll around. Health issues have sidelined him in recent years.

Vince Tenuto, the Daley loyalist, driver and volunteer, began a new career after Richard M. Daley was elected mayor. He became a manager in the city's Department of Streets and Sanitation and he worked well past the age of seventy. He ran a popular St. Joseph's table event every year on March 19, attended by politicians and city workers, with proceeds going to local charities. Every day, in his office he lights a candle to St. Joseph, and visitors sometimes place written petitions underneath it, prayers for a relative who is sick or someone who has died. The petitions have accumulated over the years and they include one for Vince's own son, Nicky, who was killed in an auto accident in 1988 at the age of thirty.

Steven Flowers worked on the 1987 reelection campaign of Harold Washington when Harold defeated Edward Vrdolyak. Flowers thought that campaign was dirtier than the first. Twenty years after Harold Washington's death, there was an interfaith religious service at the Chicago Temple commemorating the anniversary. The crowd was not large, but the *Chicago Tribune* reported that nearly everyone there had a personal memory of Washington. Steven Flowers said, "He was my greatest birthday present. I turned thirty on April 12, 1983." Today, Steven Flowers is a clinical social worker.

Philip Krone, the master political consultant who helped steer the political career of Richard M. Daley for so many years, died of cancer in August of 2010. He was sixty-nine years old and working the phones until the end. An obituary said his memorial service was being postponed until after the November elections.

Tom Manion, the North Side organizer for Daley, is a businessman and sometimes political consultant today. He did the same work when Daley finally won in 1989. But he has fond memories of the campaign of 1983. "It was by far the most fun campaign I worked in. The people I worked with are still my best friends. There was nothing in it for anybody. They were just a bunch of volunteers and they gave their blood, sweat and tears for this guy. And it was just one helluva fun campaign."[9]

John Deardourff, the pioneer political consultant who invented the "Epton, before it's too late" campaign, died of cancer in 2004 in McLean, Virginia, at the age of seventy-one. Deardourff was considered one of the pioneers of the political consulting business. His partner, Doug Bailey, said, "When campaigns became so negative and the process so dominated by money in the mid to late 1980s, that was when both of us became less comfortable."

James Fletcher, who managed the Epton campaign, became one of the most successful lobbyists in Springfield. Understandably, he did not want to be interviewed for this book. He still has to deal with the Illinois Legislature and doesn't want to remind African

---

9   Tom Manion, interview.

American legislators of his role in the "Epton, before it's too late" campaign.

David Sawyer, the New York political consultant who created the new Jane Byrne and got along so well with the sometimes difficult mayor, died of a brain tumor in July of 1995 at age fifty-nine. He had been a consultant to prominent Democratic senators, including Daniel Patrick Moynihan, John Glenn and Edward Kennedy. Sawyer's wife, Nell, died of breast cancer later that same month at age fifty.

Ken Bode, the former NBC correspondent who had the Epton medical records dropped on him, became a journalism professor at Northwestern and DePauw Universities. He is now retired.

Carol Marin and Don Moseley, who aired the Epton medical records story, are still plying the journalism trade in Chicago.

Years after the election of '83, a new sheriff rode into town. His name was Patrick Fitzgerald and he wore the badge of United States Attorney for the Northern District of Illinois. Fitzgerald was a zealot and a workaholic, a scary combination. Aides began getting e-mails that were written in the middle of the night. Since there's always some type of corruption floating around Chicago, it wasn't long before the trials began.

A former governor, George Ryan, Bernie Epton's old pal, was sent to prison. Then the reform governor who replaced him was indicted for trying to sell a senate seat. He was also impeached. In 2010, he was put on trial, but a federal jury could not reach agreement on twenty-three counts of extortion and racketeering and found him guilty of one count of lying to the FBI. The feds vowed to retry him. His name is Rod Blagojevich and, for awhile, after he was thrown out of office, he became a popular television personality. His life story no doubt will one day become a movie and, if Blagojevich himself doesn't star, Jim Carrey should play the lead role.

In 2010, the city of Chicago's budget was short more than $650 million.

And who knows what will be next? What hot wind will blow in from the West, meet the cool waters of Lake Michigan and create a whirlwind? But that's Chicago.

Timeline

DECEMBER 20, 1976	Richard J. Daley dies suddenly after serving 21 years as Mayor of Chicago.
DECEMBER 28, 1975	The Chicago City Council elects Michael Bilandic as the acting Mayor.
APRIL 19, 1977	Bilandic wins a primary election to fill the unexpired term of Mayor Daley. He defeats five other Democrats including Alderman Roman Pucinski and State Senator Harold Washington.
JUNE 7, 1977	Bilandic easily wins the general election for Mayor. Only 38% of the city's eligible voters turn out.
NOVEMBER 21, 1977	Mayor Bilandic fires Jane Byrne, his Commissioner of Consumer Affairs, after she accuses him of improperly awarding fare increases to the city's taxi companies.
MARCH 1978	Jane Byrne announces she's a Democratic candidate for Mayor.
DECEMBER 31, 1978	One of the worst winter storms in Chicago's history begins and continues into the new year.
FEBRUARY 22, 1979	Jane Byrne wins the Democratic primary for Mayor of Chicago in what is described as the biggest election upset in Illinois history.
MARCH 18, 1980	Byrne-backed candidates, Senator Edward Kennedy for President and Edward Burke for Cook County State's Attorney, lose in the Illinois primary election.
MARCH 1981	Mayor Byrne and her husband move into the crime-ridden Cabrini Green public housing project.

NOVEMBER 4, 1982	State's Attorney Richard M. Daley announces his candidacy for Mayor in the Democratic primary election.
NOVEMBER 10, 1982	Congressman Harold Washington announces he will seek the Democratic nomination for Mayor of Chicago.
NOVEMBER 22, 1982	Mayor Jane Byrne announces she will seek reelection.
NOVEMBER 30, 1982	Chicago's Republican Party nominates Bernard Epton as its candidate for Mayor.
FEBRUARY 22, 1983	Congressman Harold Washington wins the Democratic primary for Mayor with 36% of the vote in a record turnout.
APRIL 12, 1983	Harold Washington narrowly defeats Bernard Epton for Mayor of Chicago after a bitter and divisive campaign.
APRIL 29, 1983	Harold Washington is sworn in as Mayor of Chicago
FEBRUARY–APRIL 1987	Harold Washington wins reelection as Mayor, defeating Jane Byrne in the primary and Aldermen Edward Vrdolyak and Donald Haider in the general election.
NOVEMBER 25, 1987	Mayor Harold Washington dies of a heart attack at age 65.
DECEMBER 13, 1987	Bernard Epton dies suddenly in Ann Arbor, Michigan. He was 66 years old.
APRIL 4, 1989	Richard M. Daley wins a special election to fill the unexpired term of Mayor Harold Washington, defeating Aldermen Edward Vrdolyak and Timothy Evans. He had earlier defeated Acting Mayor Eugene Sawyer in a primary election. Richard M. Daley goes on to serve 22 years as Mayor, breaking his father's record for time in that office.

Index

E

Eagleton, Thomas, 162
11th Ward
    and Bilandic, 27–30
    and Byrne, 49, 64
    and Richard M. Daley, 88, 130
El train. *See* Chicago Transit Authority.
Emmanuel, Rahm, 194
Epton, Arthur I., 91–93
Epton, Bernard
    and Blair, 96, 97
    in debate with Washington, 163, 164
    Democratic support of, 171, 172, 174
    early life of, 91–93
    election night interview with, 175, 176
    and Fletcher, 198
    and medical records, 159–162
    on Insurance Committee, 96, 165, 166
    Marzullo's endorsement of, 169
    police support of, 173, 174
    primary campaign, 132
    racial atmosphere and, 152, 170–173
    racial tone in campaign ads, 153, 154,
        157, 168
    replacement with Byrne, 143
    Republican support of, 98, 141, 142
    and Safire article, 168, 169
    in Saint Patrick's Day Parade, 167
    selected as candidate, 120
    as state representative, 95–97
    and Thompson, 98
    in World War II, 94
Epton, Jeff, 97, 170, 173, 191
Epton, Jerry, 93, 94, 190
Epton, Saul, 92, 160
Ewell, Raymond, 74, 75, 177, 195
Ewing, Russ, 67, 109, 110, 159, 160, 196

F

50th Ward, 64
1st Ward, 52
Fitzgerald, Patrick, 199
Fletcher, James, 153, 157, 198
Flowers, Mary, 190
Flowers, Steven, 111, 130, 139, 198
44th Ward, 40, 46
49th Ward, 130
47th Ward, 110, 122, 123

Fraternal Order of Police, 173. *See also*
    Chicago Police Department.
Freeman, Aaron, 185
Freeman, Charles, 71–73, 187
Friedman, Richard, 81, 82
Frost, Wilson, 23–25
Frumkin, Paul, 17

G

gangs, 63
gay community, 40, 41
Gleason, Bill, 134
Golden, Harry, Jr., 124, 163
Graber, Doris, 156
Green, Theophilus E., 178, 179
Griffin, Bill
    and Bilandic, 40
    and Brown, 132
    and Byrne's write-in campaign, 142
    and Continental Air Transport
        Company, 128
    and DiLeonardi, 52
    on election night, 137, 138
    hired by Byrne, 50, 119
    post-political career, 195
    and Quigley, 56, 57
    resignation of, 53
    and taxi cab fare scandal, 32, 33

H

Haider, Donald, 188, 190
Hanhardt, William, 51
Hanrahan, Edward, 85, 86
Hill, Hugh, 16, 48
Hoffman, Abbie, 14
Hoge, James, 163, 164
Holt, Lindsley "Jelly," 112, 113, 140
Hyde, Henry, 96, 97
Hynes, Thomas, 76, 188

I

Illinois House, 75, 95–97
Illinois Senate, 76, 82, 83
Independent Voters of Illinois (IVI), 29
Insurance Committee, 96
insurance industry, 96, 165, 166
Israel, 16, 17

R

Racism. *See also* African Americans.
  and Epton, 170, 171, 173, 191
  forgiveness of, 171
  and Vrdolyak, 132, 133, 135
  and Washington, 74
Raymond, Michael, 186
Reagan, Ronald, 78, 120
Redmond, William, 75
Rein, Irving, 126
Reuben, Don, 32, 33
riots, 13, 15, 95
Robb, Charles, 154
Robinson, Renault, 114–116, 119, 125,
    187, 197
Rohr, Charles E. "Bud," 94
Roosevelt University, 72
Rose, Don, 46–48, 86, 156, 196
Rostenkowski, Dan, 28
Roti, Fred, 52, 63
Royko, Mike
  and Bailey-Deardourff, 154
  and Bilandic, 30, 32
  and Byrne, 61
  closing of *Chicago Daily News,* 37
  election analysis, 137
  Epton's view of, 176
  and Richard J. Daley, 14, 21, 22
  and Richard M. Daley, 87, 88
  on Washington's victory, 141
Ryan, George, 191

S

Safire, William, 168, 169
Sain, Kenneth, 25
Saint Pascal's Catholic Church, 155–157
Saint Patrick's Day Parade, 57, 166, 167
Sawyer, David, 119, 120, 138, 142, 199
Sawyer, Eugene, 193
scandal, 127. *See also* corruption.
schools, 59, 61
Sheahan, James "Skinny," 105–107, 123,
    124, 134, 135, 196
Sheahan, Mike, 105, 106
shoot-to-kill, 13
Simon, Roger, 176
Singer, William, 30, 46, 105
Sinatra, Frank, 20

Spilotro, "Tony the Ant," 63
Stevenson, Adlai, 120, 121
Stewart, Bennett, 77
Straza, Wayne, 187
Streets and Sanitation Department of, 36,
    130, 197
Stricklin, Jim, 107, 108, 152, 176, 189, 196
Sullivan, Frank, 20, 24
Swibel, Charlie, 128

T

taxi cab fares, 31–33
Tenuto, Vince, 108, 109, 138, 197
Teramino, Tony, 123
Terkel, Studs, 173
3rd Ward, 71, 72, 77, 112, 113
13th Ward, 123, 124, 135
35th Ward, 151
Thomas, Danny, 94, 96
Thompson, James R., 98, 120, 121,
    141–143
Travis, Dempsey, 70, 188
Tucker, Robert, 29
29th Ward, 71, 174

V

Vietnam War, 12, 19, 97, 160
vote fraud, 177
voter registration, 121, 129
Vrdolyak, Edward
  and Byrne, 47
  after Daley's death, 23–25
  indictment of, 194, 195
  and Lindsey, 122
  and Washington, 132, 135, 172,
    184–188
Vuckovich, D.M., 174

W

walk around money, 177, 178
Walker Commission Report, 15
Wall, Rev. James, 55
Walsh, Ed, 64
Walton, James, 71
Washington, Harold
  African American support of, 118, 121,
    129, 130, 133, 171, 177–179

About the Author

A NATIVE OF BUFFALO, NY, Peter Nolan arrived in Chicago near the end of the turbulent 1960's. He worked in television news as a writer, reporter and commentator and won three Emmys and several journalism awards.

He lives in the Chicago suburb of Glenview and has six children and fifteen grandchildren.

Made in the USA
Lexington, KY
21 October 2012